Measuring User Engagement

Synthesis Lectures on Information Concepts, Retrieval, and Services

Editor
Gary Marchionini, *University of North Carolina, Chapel Hill*

Synthesis Lectures on Information Concepts, Retrieval, and Services is edited by Gary Marchionini of the University of North Carolina. The series will publish 50- to 100-page publications on topics pertaining to information science and applications of technology to information discovery, production, distribution, and management. The scope will largely follow the purview of premier information and computer science conferences, such as ASIST, ACM SIGIR, ACM/IEEE JCDL, and ACM CIKM. Potential topics include, but are not limited to: data models, indexing theory and algorithms, classification, information architecture, information economics, privacy and identity, scholarly communication, bibliometrics and webometrics, personal information management, human information behavior, digital libraries, archives and preservation, cultural informatics, information retrieval evaluation, data fusion, relevance feedback, recommendation systems, question answering, natural language processing for retrieval, text summarization, multimedia retrieval, multilingual retrieval, and exploratory search.

Measuring User Engagement
Mounia Lalmas, Heather O'Brien, and Elad Yom-Tov
2014

The Taxobook: History, Theories, and Concepts of Knowledge Organization
Marjorie Hlava
2014

Children's Internet Search: Using Roles to Understand Children's Search Behavior
Elizabeth Foss and Allison Druin
2014

Digital Library Technologies: Complex Objects, Annotation, Ontologies, Classification, Extraction, and Security
Edward A. Fox and Ricardo da Silva Torres
2014

Digital Libraries Applications: CBIR, Education, Social Networks, eScience/Simulation, and GIS
Edward A. Fox and Jonathan P. Leidig
2014

Information and Human Values
Kenneth R. Fleischmann
2013

Multiculturalism and Information and Communication Technology
Pnina Fichman and Madelyn R. Sanfilippo
2013

Transforming Technologies to Manage Our Information: The Future of Personal Information Management, Part II
William Jones
2013

Designing for Digital Reading
Jennifer Pearson, George Buchanan, and Harold Thimbleby
2013

Information Retrieval Models: Foundations and Relationships
Thomas Roelleke
2013

Key Issues Regarding Digital Libraries: Evaluation and Integration
Rao Shen, Marcos Andre Goncalves, and Edward A. Fox
2013

Visual Information Retrieval using Java and LIRE
Mathias Lux and Oge Marques
2013

On the Efficient Determination of Most Near Neighbors: Horseshoes, Hand Grenades, Web Search and Other Situations When Close is Close Enough
Mark S. Manasse
2012

The Answer Machine
Susan E. Feldman
2012

Theoretical Foundations for Digital Libraries: The 5S (Societies, Scenarios, Spaces, Structures, Streams) Approach
Edward A. Fox, Marcos André Gonçalves, and Rao Shen
2012

The Future of Personal Information Management, Part I: Our Information, Always and Forever
William Jones
2012

Search User Interface Design
Max L. Wilson
2011

Information Retrieval Evaluation
Donna Harman
2011

Knowledge Management (KM) Processes in Organizations: Theoretical Foundations and Practice
Claire R. McInerney and Michael E. D. Koenig
2011

Search-Based Applications: At the Confluence of Search and Database Technologies
Gregory Grefenstette and Laura Wilber
2010

Information Concepts: From Books to Cyberspace Identities
Gary Marchionini
2010

Estimating the Query Difficulty for Information Retrieval
David Carmel and Elad Yom-Tov
2010

iRODS Primer: Integrated Rule-Oriented Data System
Arcot Rajasekar, Reagan Moore, Chien-Yi Hou, Christopher A. Lee, Richard Marciano, Antoine de Torcy, Michael Wan, Wayne Schroeder, Sheau-Yen Chen, Lucas Gilbert, Paul Tooby, and Bing Zhu
2010

Collaborative Web Search: Who, What, Where, When, and Why
Meredith Ringel Morris and Jaime Teevan
2009

Multimedia Information Retrieval
Stefan Rüger
2009

Online Multiplayer Games
William Sims Bainbridge
2009

Information Architecture: The Design and Integration of Information Spaces
Wei Ding and Xia Lin
2009

Reading and Writing the Electronic Book
Catherine C. Marshall
2009

Hypermedia Genes: An Evolutionary Perspective on Concepts, Models, and Architectures
Nuno M. Guimarães and Luís M. Carrico
2009

Understanding User-Web Interactions via Web Analytics
Bernard J. (Jim) Jansen
2009

XML Retrieval
Mounia Lalmas
2009

Faceted Search
Daniel Tunkelang
2009

Introduction to Webometrics: Quantitative Web Research for the Social Sciences
Michael Thelwall
2009

Exploratory Search: Beyond the Query-Response Paradigm
Ryen W. White and Resa A. Roth
2009

New Concepts in Digital Reference
R. David Lankes
2009

Automated Metadata in Multimedia Information Systems: Creation, Refinement, Use in Surrogates, and Evaluation
Michael G. Christel
2009

Measuring User Engagement

Mounia Lalmas, Heather O'Brien, and Elad Yom-Tov

ISBN: 978-3-031-01161-0   paperback
ISBN: 978-3-031-02289-0   ebook

DOI 10.1007/978-3-031-02289-0

A Publication in the Springer series
SYNTHESIS LECTURES ON INFORMATION CONCEPTS, RETRIEVAL, AND SERVICES

Lecture #38
Series Editor: Gary Marchionini, *University of North Carolina, Chapel Hill*
Series ISSN
Print 1947-945X   Electronic 1947-9468

Measuring User Engagement

Mounia Lalmas
Yahoo Labs

Heather O'Brien
University of British Columbia

Elad Yom-Tov
Microsoft Research

*SYNTHESIS LECTURES ON INFORMATION CONCEPTS, RETRIEVAL,
AND SERVICES #38*

ABSTRACT

User engagement refers to the quality of the user experience that emphasizes the positive aspects of interacting with an online application and, in particular, the desire to use that application longer and repeatedly. User engagement is a key concept in the design of online applications (whether for desktop, tablet or mobile), motivated by the observation that successful applications are not just used, but are engaged with. Users invest time, attention, and emotion in their use of technology, and seek to satisfy pragmatic and hedonic needs.

Measurement is critical for evaluating whether online applications are able to successfully engage users, and may inform the design of and use of applications. User engagement is a multi-faceted, complex phenomenon; this gives rise to a number of potential measurement approaches. Common ways to evaluate user engagement include using self-report measures, e.g., questionnaires; observational methods, e.g. facial expression analysis, speech analysis; neuro-physiological signal processing methods, e.g., respiratory and cardiovascular accelerations and decelerations, muscle spasms; and web analytics, e.g., number of site visits, click depth. These methods represent various trade-offs in terms of the setting (laboratory versus "in the wild"), object of measurement (user behaviour, affect or cognition) and scale of data collected. For instance, small-scale user studies are deep and rich, but limited in terms of generalizability, whereas large-scale web analytic studies are powerful but negate users' motivation and context.

The focus of this book is how user engagement is currently being measured and various considerations for its measurement. Our goal is to leave readers with an appreciation of the various ways in which to measure user engagement, and their associated strengths and weaknesses. We emphasize the multifaceted nature of user engagement and the unique contextual constraints that come to bear upon attempts to measure engagement in different settings, and across different user groups and web domains. At the same time, this book advocates for the development of "good" measures and good measurement practices that will advance the study of user engagement and improve our understanding of this construct, which has become so vital in our wired world.

KEYWORDS

user engagement, user experience, methods, measurement, online activity, eye tracking, loyalty, mouse tracking, popularity, physiological measurement, self-report measurement, web analytics, intra-session, inter-session, reliability and validity, multitasking, dwell time, mixed methods

Contents

Preface . . . . **xiii**

Acknowledgments . . . . **xv**

1 Introduction and Scope **1**
   1.1   Definitions 2
   1.2   User Engagement vs. User Experience 3
   1.3   Characteristics 4
       1.3.1 Focused Attention 4
       1.3.2 Positive Affect 4
       1.3.3 Aesthetics Appeal 5
       1.3.4 Endurability 5
       1.3.5 Novelty 5
       1.3.6 Richness and Control 6
       1.3.7 Reputation, Trust, and Expectation 6
       1.3.8 User Context, Motivation, Incentives, and Benefits 7
   1.4   Measurements 7
   1.5   Scope 10
   1.6   Structure 10

2 Approaches Based on Self-Report Methods **11**
   2.1   Self-Report Approaches 12
   2.2   Advantages and Limitations of Self-Report Methods 12
       2.2.1 Communication 13
       2.2.2 Methodology Bias 13
       2.2.3 Reliability and Validity 14
   2.3   Interviews 15
       2.3.1 Types of Interviews 15
       2.3.2 Applying Interviews to Measure User Engagement 16
   2.4   Think Aloud and Think After Protocols 18
       2.4.1 Think Aloud 18
       2.4.2 Think After 19

      2.4.3 Relationship to User Engagement 20

2.5   Questionnaires 20

2.6   Questionnaires for Measuring User Engagement 22

      2.6.1 Survey to Evaluate Engagement 22

      2.6.2 Engagement and Influences on Questionnaire 23

      2.6.3 User Engagement Scale 24

      2.6.4 eHealth Engagement Scale 26

2.7   Constructs Related to User Engagement 27

      2.7.1 Mental Workload 27

      2.7.2 Disorientation 27

      2.7.3 Playfulness 28

      2.7.4 Cognitive Absorption 29

2.8   Summary 29

3   Approaches Based on Physiological Measurements 31

3.1   Psychophysiological Measurements 32

3.2   Facial Expressions 34

3.3   Eye Tracking 35

      3.3.1 Eye Tracking and Search 36

      3.3.2 Eye Tracking and Reading 36

      3.3.3 Eye Tracking and Selection 37

      3.3.4 Summary and Limitations 38

3.4   Cursor Tracking 38

      3.4.1 Aligning Eye Gaze and Mouse Movement 39

      3.4.2 Mouse Movement in Search 41

      3.4.3 Mouse Movement Elsewhere 43

3.5   Summary 44

4   Approaches Based on Web Analytics 47

4.1   Intra-Session vs. Inter-Session Engagement 47

4.2   Some Dimensions of Online Measurements 48

      4.2.1 Dependence on the Type of Website 48

      4.2.2 Dependence on the Type of User 49

      4.2.3 Dependence on the Task 50

4.3   Large-Scale Measurements 50

4.4   Intra-Session Measurements 52

      4.4.1 Dwell Time and Similar Measures 52

          4.4.2 Revisits to a Site 54
          4.4.3 Clickthrough Rate... 55
          4.4.4 Number of Pages Viewed 55
          4.4.5 Other Measurements 56
    4.5 Inter-Session Measurements 56
          4.5.1 Direct Value Measurement 57
          4.5.2 Total Use Measurement 57
          4.5.3 Return-Rate Measurement 58
    4.6 Summary 58

5 Beyond Desktop, Single Site, and Single Task **61**
    5.1 Measuring for Online Multitasking................................. 61
    5.2 Measuring on a Network of Sites................................... 64
    5.3 Measuring in Mobile Information Seeking 68
    5.4 Summary 71

6 Enhancing the Rigor of User Engagement Methods and Measures **73**
    6.1 Scale 74
    6.2 Setting 76
    6.3 Temporality 78
    6.4 Objectivity and Subjectivity 81
    6.5 Process- and Product-Based.. 84
    6.6 Summary 85

7 Conclusions and Future Research Directions **87**
    7.1 Summary 87
    7.2 Future Research Directions 88
    7.3 Take-Aways 90

Bibliography **93**

Authors' Biographies **113**

Index **115**

Preface

User engagement is not a new concept, but has bubbled to the surface over the past decade, attracting a number of academic and industry researchers from diverse fields, including information, computer, and learning sciences. We live in a highly connected society, as evidenced from the plethora of web-ready devices and how these have been integrated into our everyday work and personal lives. Engaging the user has become a goal—and to some extent, a necessity—for online search companies, e-commerce firms, news portals, etc. and a source of interest for those of us invested in understanding the relationship between people, technology and information.

A major challenge in the study of user engagement continues to be the lack of a shared definition and understanding of user engagement and its measurement. The term "user engagement" is frequently referred to as a desired outcome of people's interactions with information technology, but this means different things to different people; many people use the term without articulating their definition. This creates further dilemmas when we turn to measurement: if we cannot define user engagement, then how do we know whether we have actually measured it?

Our impetus in writing this book was to shed light on these challenges, but also to highlight important existing and emerging work in this area. Although our focus here is on measurement, we ground the book by first defining user engagement and its characteristics. We also list important measurement attributes, such as scale and temporality. These measurement attributes are used to frame our discussion and to encourage researchers to consider factors of scale, time, etc. when determining their approach to measurement in a given context.

We then move into describing three approaches: self-report, web analytics, and physiological methods. In this book, we devote a chapter to each of these approaches. These chapters focus specifically on how self-report, web analytics, and physiological methods have been employed to measure engagement, and their advantages and limitations. Self-report approaches rely on asking users about their experiences though questionnaires, interviews, and so on. Alternatively, physiological measures, which can track user gaze and mouse movements can be performed in the lab and, increasingly, by Internet companies. The latter, however, still mostly relies on web analytic approaches such as calculating dwell time and return rate.

In the final chapters of the book, we share emerging measurement techniques in the areas of mobile search, the networked environment and multi-tasking. In doing so, we push the measurement agenda for user engagement "beyond the desktop, a single site, and a single task" to more closely reflect the ways in which technology users are interacting with web applications and their use of different devices to do so. We conclude by returning to the measurement attributes, and discuss these with respect to enhancing the rigor of measurement application.

This book makes strong references to our own work and relies on the expertise we have developed working in this area. It takes years to properly understand and talk confidently about what user engagement is, what it is not, and what a particular measurement tells us about it. Particularly important for us was to present the three main types of approaches in detail to fully comprehend what each can bring to the study of user engagement. Combining approaches will allow for a richer and deeper understanding of what user engagement is, how to measure it properly, and how to interpret the measurement outcomes to then be able to act upon them in an informed manner.

Our belief is that this text will provide a solid foundation for defining and measuring user engagement in both research and application. It is our intention to promote an active and robust agenda for user engagement and its measurement across various fields of inquiry.

Mounia Lalmas, Heather O'Brien, and Elad Yom-Tov
November 2014

Acknowledgments

This book was written as a result of the tutorial "Measuring User Engagement" given at the World Wide Wide (WWW) Conference 2013, Rio de Janeiro. The slides are available at `http://www.slideshare.net/mounialalmas/measuring-userengagement`. We would like to thank the WWW organizers for making our tutorial a success, as we received many positive feedbacks and ideas to improve its content and as a result the scope of this book.

Mounia Lalmas would like to thank her colleagues at Yahoo for their various feedbacks on several versions of this book. She is also very much in debt to her "two boys," Thomas and Leon, for providing her glasses of wines in the evening and ensuring she remained an "OK mummy."

Heather O'Brien would like to thank the students and colleagues that have challenged her and inspired her over the past several years to continue on this "user engagement journey," and her family (Paul and Si) for their love and encouragement. She would also like to acknowledge the financial support of the Social Sciences and Humanities Research Council of Canada and the Networks of Excellence Graphics, Animation, and New Media project.

Various parts of this book are based on works carried with various colleagues, which we would like to acknowledge: Ioannis Arapakis ([9, 11] in Chapters 3 and 6); Simon Attfield, Gabriella Kazai, and Benjamin Piwowarski ([15] in Chapter 1); Georges Dupret ([48] in Chapters 4 and 6); Janette Lehmann ([121, 122, 211, 212] in Chapters 4 and 5); Lori McCay-Peet ([134] in Chapters 2 and 6); and David Warnock ([203] in Chapter 6).

Mounia Lalmas, Heather O'Brien, and Elad Yom-Tov
November 2014

CHAPTER 1

Introduction and Scope

The nature of human-computer interactions has dramatically changed over the past several decades. In the 1980s the dominant interaction paradigm was of a solitary individual sitting in front of one workstation, most probably in an office, manipulating the interface through a keyboard and mouse. Fast forward to the 21st century where human-computer interaction's (HCI) "third wave" [25] is dominated by discourse on User Experience (UX). UX is framed as

> "a consequence of a user's internal state (predispositions, expectations, needs, motivation, mood, etc.), the characteristics of the designed system (e.g., complexity, purpose, usability, functionality, etc.) and the context (or the environment) within which the interaction occurs (e.g., organizational/social setting, meaningfulness of the activity, voluntariness of use, etc.)." [74]

UX is an all-encompassing view of how people interact with technologies, but also how these interactions are shaped by human values, contextual constraints, and society.

Today, the emphasis on UX is one demonstration of the pervasiveness of technology in our lives, and the blurred lines between the public and private spheres. Specifically, the continually evolving web provides unprecedented choice in how we educate ourselves, buy and sell goods and services, entertain and express ourselves, communicate with family and friends, and become informed about our world. For each of these activities, there are a plethora of applications or websites to chose from: hundreds of online news providers and e-commerces sites, numerous social networking sites, dozens of general web search engines, and free email tools. In addition, the ubiquity of smartphones and tablet devices coupled with constant connectivity to the Internet allow users to learn, shop, search, play, converse, etc., whenever and wherever they wish.

In line with these changes, there is an impetus to move beyond ensuring applications are merely usable. We must consider the *hedonic and experiential* factors of interacting with technology, such as fun, fulfillment, play, and *user engagement*. As such, traditional indicators of usability—effectiveness, efficiency and satisfaction—and their associated metrics are not sufficient for capturing user experience. In the case of user engagement, let us consider "time on task." In usability research, this is an indicator of efficiency, marking the ability of a system to deliver information quickly into the user's hands. Yet user engagement sees this same measure as problematic. Does extended time on task point to an engaged or disoriented user? This example demonstrates that measuring user engagement is complex and likely requires multiple, meaningful indicators to address its affective, cognitive, and behavioral components.

The measurement of user engagement is a daunting task for all of us working in "third wave" HCI. We struggle with a range of questions: Are users' self-reports of their engagement reliable? Can we infer user engagement from physiological responses? What do behavioral patterns across millions of web searchers tell us about what engages or disengages users? What are the costs and trade-offs associated with any one methodological approach? And, in a world of rapid technological change, how do we capture engagement well enough to inform design? This latter question is fundamentally the driving force. Web developers want and need to engage users, but there are currently few guidelines (with some exceptions [191]) to channel designers' efforts to "make things engaging" [159]. In a world full of choices, failing to engage the user "equates with no sale on an electronic commerce site and no transmission of information from a website; people go elsewhere" [150]. Although designing for engagement may be the ultimate goal, it cannot be realized without a common understanding of what user engagement is and how to measure it. The focus of this book is on how user engagement is currently being measured and on present and future considerations for its measurement. It is our belief that defining and measuring user engagement form the foundation of user engagement research and design.

1.1   DEFINITIONS

The need to engage users and create engaging technologies is an oft-cited goal when developing interactive systems [159]. But what *is* engagement? The definition of user engagement has been evolving since the mid-1980s. The concept of "direct engagement" emphasized the interaction between human and machine, whereby the users' cognitive intentions could be realized through the physical manipulation of the interface [82]. Laurel made the cognitive and affective aspects of this exchange more prominent in her definition of user engagement as "the state of mind that we must attain in order to enjoy a representation of an action" so that we may experience computer worlds "directly, without mediation or distraction" [115]. Most recently, Attfield et al. [15] emphasized the positive aspects of the user experience as necessary for engagement. Another stream of definitions has been less focused on the individual user's perspective, and more on the designer's mandate. These definitions focus on the ability of the system or application to "catch and captivate user interest" [87] and attention [15], "draw people in" and "encourage interaction" [167], and "excite, motivate and enhance the user experience" [19].

In an attempt to bridge definitions from various disciplines and perspectives, O'Brien [154], drawing upon the work of Webster & Ho [206] and Jacques [87] and their colleagues, rooted user engagement in Flow, Play, and Aesthetic theories and examined a suite of attributes: challenge, aesthetic and sensory appeal, feedback, novelty, interactivity, perceived control and time, awareness, motivation, interest, and affect that characterized engaging experiences with technology [150] across disciplines and domains. She linked user engagement with user experience, specifically McCarthy and Wright's spatio-temporal, compositional, emotional, and sensual "Threads of Experience" [133] to provide a framework for thinking about user engagement.

Further, she explored distinct stages of the engagement process, from the point of engagement through sustained engagement, to disengagement and re-engagement.

One challenge is that, despite past efforts, the definition of user engagement remains "clunky" and lacks the ability to be meaningfully communicated amongst researchers and designers. However, collectively work to date points to the behavioral, cognitive, and affective components of user engagement [15, 87, 150], the fact that there are gradations of user engagement [150], and that there is a need to examine user engagement within individual sessions (engaging interaction) *and* across multiple sessions (long-term engagement). This aligns with the way the online industry includes user loyalty and retention in their assessment of user engagement. We therefore use the following definition, which distinguishes three dimensions of user engagement:

> User engagement is the *emotional, cognitive, and behavioral* experience of a user with a technological resource that exists, at any point in time *and* over time.

This definition is intentionally broad. Identifying emotional, cognitive, and behavioral factors emphasizes the holistic nature of user engagement, and is suggestive of aspects that are open to different types of measurement, as will be postulated in this book. Finally, the definition also refers equally to user engagement in terms of a single session or across multiple sessions.

1.2   USER ENGAGEMENT VS. USER EXPERIENCE

User engagement should not be confused with user experience,[1] although, as the above discussion suggests, there is a relationship between the two. UX is part of "third wave" HCI and there has been much discussion around its definition and articulating a research agenda for its pursuit [74].

A great user experience does not necessarily lead to a high level of engagement and, vice versa, high engagement does not insure a great user experience. For example, a social network such as Twitter or LinkedIn may not provide a superior user experience to, for instance Facebook or Instagram, but the nature of the engagement each facilitates (e.g., remaining informed on latest news on Twitter and keeping up with people's professional development on LinkedIn) make users access them regularly. Another example is the success of Apple, which is said to be largely attributed to how its products and services align with engaged user behavior—e.g., the "need" to download music and apps.

User engagement manifests in how people choose to get value from the user experience, as enabled by the application (e.g., social network) and device (e.g., smartphone) they elect to use. In other words, user engagement represents the purposeful choices users make to get what they want and, as such, has a more restricted meaning that focuses on the quality of the experience. It is this quality that will make a technology engaging, in particular for long-term interactions.

---

[1]See the HBR Blog Network at http://blogs.hbr.org/2012/12/dont-confuse-engagement-with-u, upon which this section is based.

1.3   CHARACTERISTICS

There is general consensus that engagement may be operationalized in terms of various attributes. An attribute is defined as "a characteristic of the user-computer interaction that influences or is a component of the engagement" [150]. O'Brien [150, 154] found commonalities for the following attributes across gaming, learning, online shopping, and web searching applications: aesthetic appeal, attention, challenge, endurability, feedback, interactivity, perceived user control, pleasure, sensory appeal, and variety/novelty; many of these were also proposed by [87] and [206] specifically in the area of educational multimedia. These attributes were expanded upon by [15] to include reputation, trust, and expectation. All of these attributes correspond to the notion of user engagement as encompassing affective, cognitive, and behavioral dimensions. While some of the characteristics have stronger ties with one of these dimensions, many are a combination of the three. Here we expand upon these engagement attributes. It should also be kept in mind that these attributes are not binary, but rather they vary in depth and extent depending on the salience of the attributes to the user-system interaction at any given point in time.

1.3.1   FOCUSED ATTENTION

Being engaged may involve being focused to the exclusion of other activities [150]. This phenomenon relates to distortions in the subjective perception of time during an interaction [151], which has been shown to be a good indicator of cognitive involvement [16], which is also linked to game immersion [89]. The more engaged users are, the more likely they are to underestimate the passage of time. High degrees of concentration, absorption, and distortion in the subjective passage of time have demonstrated the connection of engagement to Flow Theory [44], where flow refers to a mental state in which users are fully immersed in what they are doing.

Measuring focused attention, or assessing the extent to which users are focused while interacting with a technology, may be complex in situations where users are engaging in routine activities, such as reading news online or checking their social network updates. In these cases, users are not likely to be totally immersed in their activities. However, in a game scenario, players become focused on the characters, quests, game environment, etc. Thus it is important when measuring focused attention to account for the type of engagement being assessed (e.g., playing a game versus reading a news article) and the expected outcomes (e.g., total immersion or flow versus loyalty).

1.3.2   POSITIVE AFFECT

Affect relates to the emotions experienced during an interaction: "Engaged users are affectively involved" [150]. For instance, a lack of enjoyment may be barrier to shopping engagement, while fun experienced during an online learning session may work to draw users in [150]. Positive affect in early encounters with a technology can act as a hook and induce a desire for exploration and discovery [90]. This itself can encourage greater emotional involvement and contribute to user loyalty. Affective states that are pertinent to user engagement include enjoyment and fun; negative emotions, such as frustration may bring about disengagement [150].

1.3.3 AESTHETICS APPEAL

Aesthetic appeal concerns the sensory and visual appeal of an interface and is seen as an important factor for engagement [151]. In the context of online shopping, web searching, educational webcasting and video games, aesthetics was shown to manifest in an application's screen layout, graphics and use of design principles, e.g., symmetry and balance [150], as previously investigated [116, 198]. In the context of multimedia applications, aesthetics (in this case media quality) has been shown to relate to positive affect [90]. It has also been suggested that aesthetics promoted focused attention and stimulated curiosity. For example, Lindgaard et al. [124] showed how quickly users judge websites in deciding whether to engage with them or move on.

A great deal of HCI research has investigated the link between usability and aesthetic appeal. For example, Tractinsky [198], in an experiment involving Automated Teller Machines, found a positive correlation between perceived usability and aesthetic appeal, though there was no relationship between perceived usability and actual usability. While this research showed a powerful link between how users perceive the functionality of the system based on its appearance, it also has an important implication for measurement—the incongruence between user perceptions and their successful use of an application. However, aesthetics should not be confused with usability; aesthetics goes beyond usability. User engagement should not be measured when an application is badly designed from a usability perspective. Understanding how aesthetics affects user engagement makes sense only when users are able to perform their tasks without hindrance.

1.3.4 ENDURABILITY

Endurability builds upon the idea that engaging experiences are memorable and worth repeating. This attribute of engagement refers to the likelihood to return to an application in the future and to share the experience of using it with others [170]. It has been operationalized as users' perceptions of whether the experience met their expectations of being successful, rewarding, or worthwhile and their willingness to recommend it to others [151]. In the context of the online news, endurability relates to the notion of "sticky" content and the aim of maintaining users' attention and encouraging them to return to the site at a future time. Having fun on a photo sharing platform, being rewarded with incentives in a community Question & Answer system, and discovering something new in a social media forum have been shown to promote endurability [150]. It is intrinsically linked to the idea of loyalty, which relates to how regularly users return to a website or an application.

1.3.5 NOVELTY

Systems may be engaging when they present users with the novel, surprising, unfamiliar, or unexpected. Novelty appeals to our sense of curiosity, encourages inquisitive behavior, and promotes re-engagement [151]. The novelty of an interaction may be situationally dependent. It may arise through the freshness of content in an online news site, or the innovativeness of the technology itself [163]. In e-commerce applications, for example, shoppers may enjoy the experience of becoming sidetracked, and browse just to see what is there [150]. It has been shown that learners experience higher levels of engagement during multimedia presentations that exhibit higher levels of variety [206].

However, it is important to balance novelty and familiarity. For example, in the context of online news, users expect fresh content on a regular basis; the same users would not be thrilled if their email tool changed dramatically every month. In gaming, the level of novelty can determine whether engagement is sustained [150], although some familiarity with a game environment can lead to faster engagement [181], reduced disorientation [206], and ultimately keep users engaged over a longer period of time.

1.3.6   RICHNESS AND CONTROL

The "Richness, Control and Engagement" framework [177] explains levels of engagement in terms of the levels of richness and control that are associated with both the features of an application and user's expertise. Richness captures how the activity of a user can grow by assessing the variety and complexity of thoughts, actions, and perceptions evoked during the activity (e.g., variety, possibilities, enjoyment, excitement, challenge) [206]; richness is closely associated with novelty. Control is the extent to which a person is able to achieve this growth potential by assessing the effort in the selection and attainment of goals (clarity, ease, self-confidence, freedom).

Imagine a child playing a computer game. Richness is what makes the game fun and challenging and what keeps that child engaged. But he or she must experience some control—otherwise the child will find the game too complex and simply abandon it. While we may all enjoy rich experiences when using a web application, we still want to have some control over it. For instance, we may enjoy the use of multimedia, i.e., video and audio, in the presentation of online news, yet prefer to engage only with text-based stories depending on time or physical constraints.

1.3.7   REPUTATION, TRUST, AND EXPECTATION

Trust is a necessary condition of user engagement. Reputation can be seen as the trust users invest globally in a given resource or provider. Trust depends on implicit contracts between people, computers, and organizations [100]. When users interact with each other, the reputation of the website has a strong influence upon the extent to which users trust each other in their transactions, e.g., on eBay [141]. Similarly, the perceived fairness of the scoring system in a question & answer (Q&A) site influences users' trust in the service and their willingness to engage with it [118]. In social networks, trust naturally has an additional dimension related to the perception of trustworthiness of user-generated content [65]. Trust can also be related to user engagement with web search services, where authoritativeness and popularity features are used to rank search results [94].

Finally, a consequence of trust or reputation is expectation, which influences engagement before a user has even reached a website [182]. We may have totally different expectations when we visit Wikipedia compared to when we visit a community Q&A system in terms of the credibility and authority of content presented in each system. Trust, reputation, and expectation have an effect on whether we wish to engage with an application over the longer-term, and the level to which we decide to engage.

1.3.8 USER CONTEXT, MOTIVATION, INCENTIVES, AND BENEFITS

We use a technology or an application, such as a website, for multiple reasons. We may need to perform work-related tasks (e.g., filling up an expense claim form) or other, mostly obligatory, duties (e.g., paying a bill, applying for a passport). On the other hand, we may decide to spend time on particular websites because we are intrinsically motivated by the desire to stay up-to-date on current events, satisfy our curiosity with information, or stay in touch with our friends and colleagues. There can also be both incentives (e.g., gaining higher status or points by answering questions on community Q&A systems) and benefits (e.g., remaining informed about the latest news) for users to engage with a technology.

Users' motivations, and the incentives and benefits offered by a system or application strongly affect how users experience and hence engage with a technology. Obviously, user experience is context dependent [117]: the experience and, as a consequence, engagement with the same tool in different circumstances (time of the day, devices used, time availability) will often be different. This means that observing user behavior over a single session may be limiting in terms of evaluating engagement [155]. Similarly, the range of available choices, as well as accepted social norms, values, and trends may impact user engagement [151]. The user's personal preferences and priorities over aspects that influence engagement, such as trendiness, coolness, or fun are likely to change in different usage scenarios and domains. In addition, different forms of engagement are likely to suit different types of personalities (e.g., couch potatoes, critics, or creators).

1.4 MEASUREMENTS

User engagement is a multifaceted, complex phenomenon with emotional, cognitive, and behavioral dimensions. This gives rise to a number of potential approaches for its measurement, including:

- *Self-reporting* through questionnaires, surveys, and interviews; we present this type of measurement in Chapter 2.

- *Physiological approaches*, which include observational methods, such as facial expression analysis, speech analysis, and desktop actions; and neuro-physiological signal processing methods, such as respiratory and cardiovascular accelerations and decelerations, and muscle spasms; these are described in Chapter 3.

- *Web analytics*, which include online behavioral metrics, including clickthrough rates, number of page views, time spent on a site (i.e., dwell time), frequency of return visits, etc. These may be collected during a single session and across several sessions.[2] This type of measurement is presented in Chapter 4.

There are a number of *dimensions* of measurement that should be considered in any methodological discussion, namely scale, setting, temporality, objectivity, and the unit of measurement. Here we briefly describe what we mean by each of these in terms of investigating user engagement:

- *Scale* refers to the size of the study, and may range from a handful of individuals participating in a diary, interview, or eye-tracking study, to hundreds of people responding to an online survey, to thousands of searchers documented through web analytics.

- *Setting* may be "in the wild" or in the laboratory. Laboratory studies may be necessary to observe behaviors directly, particularly if eye tracking or physiological sensors are the preferred way of recording this behavior. They also allow researchers to maintain a higher level of consistency and control, which enhances the internal validity of the research. However, studies conducted "in the wild" or field will have greater external validity and be more "true to life." Examples range from collecting and analyzing log file data to conducting ethnographic research in participants' homes or workplaces.

- By *temporality* we mean the "snapshot" of user engagement, in terms of whether it is short-term or long-term. In both of these cases, we must consider whether the timeframe is capturing single individuals in one or multiple sessions, or all activity on a particular website within a period of a few hours or several weeks. In other words, the user, the web application, or both may be the unit of analysis.

- *Objectivity* is a challenging term, as it is sometimes used to infer the "truthfulness" of conclusions reached by the measurement. For our purposes, we use the definition of subjectivity as the "internal, psychological world" of research participants, such as an account obtained through self-reporting, and objectivity to mean the things "external" to the psychology of the user, such as web log behavior [72].

- In the case of user engagement, the *unit of measurement* may be process-based or product based:

  - By process-based, we mean the data points collected over time. For example, we might be interested in how individual skin conductance levels (a physiological measure associated with affect) change over the course of interacting with a news website when

---

[2]With the explosion of user-generated content, socio-metrics, which include the number of comments, social networking sites' (e.g., Facebook) "like" buttons and Twitter re-tweets are also becoming standard measures of website performance (in particular for news websites) [17, 41, 101]. In this book, we do not consider socio-metrics.

viewing positive and negative content, or we might examine clickthrough patterns of a particular website across thousands of its users. With process-based measures, the intention is to discover where a behavioral, cognitive, or affective change occurred during the course of interacting with an application.

- Product-based or outcome measures are usually summative in nature. We might use a questionnaire or think-after protocol to ask searchers about their experiences after the fact, or we might calculate totals based on process measures, such as the overall number of clicks, dwell time, etc. Product-based measures are useful for trying to elicit feedback from users in their own words, or for the purposes of comparing web applications, for instance, which travel website has the greatest bounce rate.

Within the following chapters, these ideas of objectivity and subjectivity, scale, temporality, setting, and process and product will be touched upon as they relate to self-report, physiological, and web analytics approaches to measuring user engagement.

We wish to emphasize that no methodological approach or measure is perfect. Indeed, the use of any one approach represents a trade-off in terms of the scale of data analyzed (ten versus ten million people) and the depth of understanding that can be achieved. For instance, collecting large-scale clickthrough data may give the researcher a fairly accurate picture of which e-commerce websites are more engaging in terms of usage, clickthrough to sale, and repeated visits, but not the reason for their success in terms of why users are drawn to their products or site designs. A small-scale study with fifty web searchers will be limited in terms of generalizability, but will provide rich insights into participants' motivations to complete search tasks or their personal qualities, e.g., level of prior knowledge with the topic area, that led to them to be more engaged with one website over another. The research questions and constraints must be weighed in the selection of any methodological approach.

Furthermore, measures of user engagement are still in their infancy. There is a hesitation to trust self-report measures, and instead use behavioral and physiological data as proxies for internal states [84]. However, this raises the question of what objective phenomena are indicative of engagement. For example, time on task has been shown to be a poor indicator of user engagement, so what behavioral measures are indicative of engagement? When it comes to physiological arousal, how do we interpret the peaks and valleys relative to engagement? Whether we are studying user engagement through self-report, physiological, or web analytics we must be aware of the biases and limitations of each, and work to establish the reliability and validity of all measures. This underscores the need to establish the sensitivity of various measures across online domains, and to work toward the development of guidelines that can be effectively referenced and practiced.

Another issue is that user engagement is a multifaceted concept. Some methods of data collection may be appropriate for studying specific attributes of engagement but not others. For example, eye tracking can capture both pupil movement and dilation. Pupil movement may be useful for identifying scanning patterns or areas of interest on the interface, which we could use as an indication of focused attention; pupil dilation is associated with arousal, another indicator of engagement. Thus a method like eye tracking has multiple measures that can serve as indicators for different attributes of user engagement. Similarly, we can think of different measures across mixed methods that might map onto attributes of user engagement. What are the best measures for capturing these attributes? More importantly, how do they work together to create a holistic picture of the phenomenon?

1.5   SCOPE

We have briefly discussed how user engagement has been defined and operationalized through its attributes. As we move forward into the next chapters, it is important to state what this book is not about. We describe how user engagement is measured for online applications that are properly designed. We do not provide guidelines for how to design engaging websites (see [191] for more on this topic), although the interpretation of user engagement metrics may inform design.

We describe the measurement of user engagement with respect to applications that users choose to engage with. Engagement with respect to mandatory applications, such as those for work purposes, may be totally different. We also focus on applications that are widely used on a regular basis, not restricted to any particular group of people, and that promote "normal" interaction, such as daily habits (reading news online, doing emails, sharing on social networks). For example, user engagement in the game industry is different; there, successful engagement means that users are totally immersed in their activity [89], which should not be compared with a daily activity such as reading news. Finally, although we may refer to specific sites or types of applications, as reported in the literature or for illustration purposes, our aim is to remain as generic as possible.

We do not claim to provide an "exhaustive" account of all existing works on user engagement; rather we report and analyze work that we have encountered and been influenced by. Finally, this book is not about "how" to influence user engagement. Our focus is on its measurement and its proper interpretation.

1.6   STRUCTURE

The book continues with three chapters, Chapters 2 to 4, describing self-report measures, physiological measures, and web analytics, respectively. Each chapter provides a detailed understanding of each type of approach, including methodological aspects, associated findings, and advantages and disadvantages. The next two chapters (Chapters 5 and 6) look distinctly at user engagement in mobile information searching and across websites, and the combination of multiple methodological approaches. The purpose of Chapter 5 is to acknowledge the complexity of user engagement in the ubiquitous computing environment, whereas Chapter 6 discusses mixed methods, with attention to issues of reliability and validity. We conclude in Chapter 7 with open research problems, and suggestions for future research directions.

CHAPTER 2

Approaches Based on Self-Report Methods

One way to measure user engagement is to ask people about their experiences. Self-reports, typically drawn from interviews, questionnaires, diaries, etc., garner users' perceptions of digital media (was it useful? was the interface attractive? was it intuitive to navigate?), but also users' perceptions of how they felt or what they thought during or after the interaction. The inherent value of self-reports for user engagement is that subjective experiences matter. Regardless of whether objective measures indicate that user engagement took place, if the user does not feel herself to be engaged then she will not evaluate the system or application positively or use it in the future.

Take the following example. A consumer spends a great deal of time browsing an online shopping website and making a purchase. Based on his actions, we might assume that he browsed leisurely, determined what he wanted to buy, and then successfully completed his transaction. Yet suppose we asked him about this experience and he relayed that this e-commerce site was the only means of obtaining the product he needed. He searched at length for what he was looking for, struggled to figure out how to add it to his shopping basket, and then took time setting up a user account to complete his purchase. Would the consumer shop here again? Not by choice. Thus if we contrast the consumer's behavior with his self-reported experience, we can see that subjective approaches provide a more holistic account of what occurred, what motivated actions and responses, and future intentions. Self-reports are a mechanism for interpreting performance measures, and may be used to identify aspects of the experience that enhanced or deterred engagement.

Self-report methods are widely used to investigate human-computer interaction phenomenon including user engagement. In addition to being the optimal choice to address some research questions, they are convenient to administer and can be applied in a variety of settings [62]. However, crafting, employing, and analyzing data from self-report measures takes time, effort, knowledge, and skill. It is not merely about "asking a bunch of questions." Care must be taken to ensure that self-report measures are robust and that they are constructed to measure what they purport to measure.

The purpose of this chapter is to explore self-report measures of user engagement, namely interviews, think aloud/think after protocols (i.e., stimulated recall), and questionnaires. First, we provide an overview of general considerations for using self-report methods, and then address interviews, stimulated recall, and questionnaires in more detail, illustrating each with concrete examples from user engagement studies.

2.1   SELF-REPORT APPROACHES

Self-report methods are designed to elicit respondents' attitudes, emotions, beliefs, and/or knowledge of a specific topic or situation. Self-reports may be designed around three approaches: discrete, dimensional, or free response. Lopatovska & Arapakis [126] provide an overview of these approaches in their synthesis of research on the study of emotion in library and information science (LIS), information retrieval (IR), and human-computer interaction (HCI).

In the discrete approach, the aim is to provide people with terms and ask them to select the ones more applicable to their situation. They may also be asked to rate the term according to intensity or duration. For example, the Positive and Negative Affect Scale (PANAS) invites respondents to rate their emotional experiences on a five-point Likert scale (where one is "very slightly or not at all" and five is "extremely"). Both positive (e.g., interested, enthusiastic) and negative (e.g., nervous, irritable) terms are included, and the aim is to determine the temporal range of the responses, e.g., "at this moment," within the past week or year, or in general [204]. The dimensional approach is a two- or three-dimensional representation of experiences, emotions, events, etc., where the phenomenon of interest is not *a priori* categories, but plotted along an anchored continuum. Two examples are semantic differential scales, and the Affect Grid, which focuses on two dimensions of emotion, pleasure-displeasure and arousal-sleepiness, is an illustration of this approach [179]. Lastly, the free response approach relies upon people to articulate phenomena in their own words (e.g., "How did you feel when you saw the error message?").

Lopatovska & Arapakis [126] articulate the benefits of each of these three approaches. For example, the discrete and dimensional approaches are efficient and generate data that can be analyzed quantitatively, while the free response approach may best capture the user's authentic voice and felt emotions or experiences. However, each approach has drawbacks. For instance, it may be challenging to analyze free response data in a quantified fashion, and discrete and dimensional approaches can present choices to participants that are limiting or difficult to interpret for their particular situation or state.

2.2   ADVANTAGES AND LIMITATIONS OF SELF-REPORT METHODS

Self-reports may be used to gauge the quality of user engagement during (i.e., in-the-moment) or after interacting with digital media. We may administer self-report measures orally or using paper- or computer-based instruments, or to individuals or groups of people. The flexibility of the setting, mode of administration, and number of concurrent users reached are some of the advantages of self-report methods. Other benefits include participant anonymity and scale [62]. An interview can provide insights into the experiences of a single user, while questionnaires function especially well for large samples, where a large number of responses can support more sophisticated statistical analysis and permit the evaluation of the questionnaire itself [62].

As with any method, there are drawbacks to self-report methods. These may be grouped according to three main themes: *communication*, *method bias*, and *reliability and validity*.

2.2.1   COMMUNICATION

General concerns revolve around the communication between researchers and participants. Communication failure may be caused by the wording of instructions or questions, the developmental stage or cognitive ability of the user (e.g., studying children's engagement with a digital library would require a different approach than investigating university students' engagement with a digital library), and the interpretation of the construct of interest. The researcher may have a different definition of a construct than the user—indeed researchers may collectively disagree about how to define a construct! Hence, consistency in defining constructs affects measurement [91]. Standardization and consensus not only improves communication with participants, but also facilitates comparison across studies.

The main challenge of self-report methods is that they typically rely upon users' recollections and/or interpretations of events. Kelly [96] notes that one of the most common issues related to self-reports is inflation where people tend to provide responses that are more positive or more frequent than reality. To illustrate, Kobayashi & Boase [104] compared mobile phone logs with self-reports of phone usage and discovered that people overestimated phone use. In another study, Junco [91] investigated college students' online activities and found discrepancies between reported and actual use of social media, email, and search engines.

2.2.2   METHODOLOGY BIAS

In addition to issues that arise in responding to self-report measures, we must also acknowledge problems inherent in the construction and administration of self-report instruments. Method bias occurs when the research methods influence the measurement of the constructs, leading to outcomes that do not reflect the actual phenomenon of interest [29]. Kelly [96] explains that method bias "is particularly problematic since it can produce results that might appear meaningful, but are only a function of the measurement technique." One way to address method bias is to employ multiple measures in a study, complementing self-reports with observational, performance and/or physiological measures. However, Burton-Jones cautions that the use of different methods may not "deal with method bias as a whole," and encourages considering the rater, the instrument, and the procedure. The rater may include the participant, researcher, or an independent inter-rater; the instrument refers to the interview protocol or interview, but also the tools used to analyze the data; and the procedure refers to all of the decisions made throughout the design and implementation of the study. By systematically addressing these three components, the researcher may be able to "identify and gradually eliminate sources of method bias over time" [29]. For example, the author [29] suggests that raters' accuracy may be improved when they have robust instruments and procedures to guide their ratings, while Kelly [96] advocates for developing standardized measures rather than creating them in an "ad hoc fashion" for each study.

2.2.3 RELIABILITY AND VALIDITY

Method bias highlights the need for well-constructed measures that have been tested for reliability and validity. At a basic level, reliable measures and methods produce consistent findings in similar circumstances. For example, if you administered a spatial ability test to a group of students one day, and to a similar group of students the following morning, and the distribution of scores was proximate, then we might conclude that the test was reliable. Validity pertains to how accurately the measure or method captures the phenomenon of interest. Internal validity is focused on what occurs during the study, whereas external validity is concerned with how well the results generalize to the real world [96]. Continuing with the above example of the spatial ability test, the internal validity of the test would be compromised if half of the students in each group filled in answers randomly. To evaluate the external validity of the test, we might send the students out into a new city with a map and calculate how long it takes them to reach specified check points. If there are correlations between the spatial ability test and the time it takes to reach check points, then we might conclude that the spatial ability test was externally valid.

Many investigations have noted the tension between reliability and validity, and that it is difficult to achieve both in the same study [96]. Precision and accuracy in measurement are not necessarily the same outcomes. Imagine that we consistently administered the spatial ability test to different groups of people and found similar distributions of scores across these samples. Now consider that we also sent each of these groups on a "map-quest," but the spatial ability test scores did not correlate with the time it took people to reach check points. In this case, we would conclude that the spatial ability test was highly reliable in that it produced consistent results with different samples and in different settings, but it was not particularly valid, since alternative measures of spatial ability failed to corroborate this measure.

Depending on the type of self-report method used, different types of reliability and validity will be considered important. For instance, in an interview study we may strive to achieve inter-rater reliability, where there is agreement amongst coders regarding the application of codes and recognition of emergent themes [96]. Inter-rater reliability may be less applicable in developing a reliable questionnaire where the desired outcome is consistency across questionnaire items (internal consistency reliability) or across administrations of the questionnaire (test-retest reliability) [164].

Similarly, validity has different dimensions, and the type of validity most salient will depend upon the research questions and desired outcomes. Content, face, or surface validity is subjective and addresses whether the measure makes sense; thus it is "socially constructed and dependent on researcher consensus" [96]. Criterion validity pertains to the relationship between the measure and other meaningful constructs [164]. For example, we might hypothesize that user engagement with a mobile app is correlated with people's confidence and skill in using their mobile devices or their attitudes toward technology adoption, i.e., trying new things. Predictive validity is the degree to which a measure predicts behavior [96]. If we asked people to rate their engagement with a website and found that those who rated it "low" never used it again while those who rated it "high" visited it regularly from that point forward, then we would say our rating mechanism had good predictive validity. Lastly construct validity represents one of the most sophisticated forms of validity and examines the extent to which a measure represents a construct, as supported by theoretical and empirical evidence [96]. This type of validity underscores the importance of building a theoretical foundation for user engagement and a body of established work in the area of measurement.

In summary, self-report measures are useful for capturing users' attitudes toward, cognitive appraisals of, and emotions surrounding their experiences of engagement with technology. The following sections focus on specific self-report methods, specifically interviews, stimulated recall, and questionnaires. We also describe how they have been employed in the measurement of user engagement and the inherent benefits and drawbacks of each for evaluating user engagement.

2.3   INTERVIEWS

"Asking questions and getting answers is a much harder task than it may seem at first. The spoken or written word always has a residue of ambiguity, no matter how carefully we word the questions and how carefully we report or code the answers. Yet interviewing is one of the most common and powerful ways in which we try to understand our fellow humans." [58]

The interview is one of the most flexible and adaptable self-report methods. Although we commonly think of interviews as face-to-face exchanges between two people, interviews may be conducted with groups of people or through other media, such as the telephone and, increasingly, the Internet (e-mail, community forums, virtual worlds, video conferencing applications, etc.). Interviews may vary in duration, frequency (one versus multiple sessions) and scope. Fontana & Frey [58] note that the interview may be used to measure a specific phenomenon, or to explore individual or group attitudes, practices, etc., in greater depth. They emphasize the active nature of the interview as a co-constructed "story" that is "shaped by the contexts and situations in which [it] takes place."

2.3.1   TYPES OF INTERVIEWS

Interviews may be *structured*, *semi-structured*, or *unstructured*. Structured interviews follow a prescribed set of questions that have limited response categories, and are therefore typically associated with surveys and opinion polls. In the structured interview, the interviewer is systematic and does not deviate from the script or share personal views or experiences with the interviewee [58]. Unstructured interviewing uses open-ended, in-depth questions and may be supplemented with participant observations. The unstructured approach is often situated in ethnographic research, where the researcher must first gain admission to the setting and locate "informants" to interview.

This involves appreciating the language or culture of the setting and working on rapport and trust with individuals within the community of interest in order to collect data [58].

Semi-structured interviews combine open- and closed-ended questions. Like structured interviews, the researcher generally follows a script or interview protocol, but it is acceptable to deviate from the order of questions, to add questions, or to ask interviewees to elaborate on their responses [128]. The interview protocol typically contains four types of questions: essential, extra, throw-away, and probing [23]. Essential questions attempt to get at the essence of the phenomenon of interest. Extra questions are similar to essential questions in terms of focus, but are worded differently for the purposes of clarifying misunderstanding with interviewees around the wording of essential questions, or acting as means of assessing the reliability of essential questions. Throw-away questions serve several purposes, including building rapport with interviewees and making them feel comfortable, and altering the pace of the interview or focus if need be. Lastly probing questions attempt to solicit more in-depth responses from interviewees, e.g., "Can you tell me more about that event?"

Determining the degree of structure to adopt in an interview study depends greatly on the purpose of the research. Guiding questions include: do we want to explore a phenomenon through brainstorming or garner feedback on an existing application or tool? Are we interested in expert opinions or user perspectives? Are we conducting the interview in the field or in a laboratory setting? How much control does the interviewer want to have during the process?

2.3.2 APPLYING INTERVIEWS TO MEASURE USER ENGAGEMENT

The use of interviews to study user engagement has tended to be exploratory in nature and used to learn more about how participants define and experience engagement with digital media.

Swift et al. [192] were interested in users' interactions with Vicotheque, a mobile application designed to foster group musical creativity. Video recorded sessions were used as data, but also to prompt participants' recall of their thought processes during the music session. Their findings focused on different types of engagement: individual, unilateral, and bilateral, based on the degree of social interactivity experienced while interacting with Vicotheque. When individuals recognized feeling engaged in the musical effects they were creating with the device, this was individual engagement. Unilateral engagement occurred when participants responded to the music effects made by others, though the person creating the effects was unaware of this attention. Lastly, bilateral engagement took place when "two participants were consciously acting and reacting to one another in dialogue." The authors favored a free response approach in the interview process due to the subjective nature of engagement; they felt making comparisons amongst participants' level of engagement with the device did not support the ultimate objective of the study, which was more descriptive in nature.

Jacques [87] began with a free response approach that culminated with a discrete approach in a series of studies. In study one, he asked people to think of two television commercials they liked and disliked, and to offer rationales for their likes and dislikes. He then sorted these free responses into ten groups, and then clustered them further into three categories: content (story-lines, players such as actors or animals); content presentation (audio or video presentation, technical quality, image, comedy, message); and effect of the commercial on the viewer (relevance to viewer, reminder, e.g., associations to other events). This method was replicated in study two, but instead of television commercials, Jacques asked participants to use a multimedia CD-ROM. In addition to soliciting likes and dislikes, he asked participants what engagement meant to them in relation to their interaction with the multimedia software. Free responses garnered in this study were compared with the categories that emerged in study one; specifically, "choice" and "control" were added to the existing list.

Study three, an experimental study, had participants performing browsing, fact finding, and information gathering tasks using an educational multimedia software. In this study, a discrete approach was employed whereby people were asked to characterize their affective response toward the software based on thirty-five emotional terms. These emotional descriptors, as well as the free response questions of what hypermedia engagement meant to participants, informed concordance analyses of the discrete terms and most frequently mentioned words in people's definitions. This study was replicated in a subsequent experiment, which asked participants to browse two different CD-ROMs and also looked at users' motivation.

These four studies culminated in Jacques' identification of six engagement attributes: attention; motivation; perceived time; control; needs (experiential and utilitarian); and attitudes (feelings). He treated these attributes as dimensions, plotting them on a continuum from low to high. For example, low motivation constitutes "little desire to continue" whereas high motivation meant there was a "willingness to continue." In addition to isolating attributes, Jacques proposed a definition of engagement as "a user's response to an interaction that gains, maintains and encourages their attention, particularly when they are intrinsically motivated" [87], and developed a thirteen-item questionnaire. This example highlights the use of interviews (sometimes in the context of an experiment) to explore user engagement for the purposes of defining a construct and creating a self-report questionnaire. Jacques also used free response, discrete, and dimensional approaches in his work to allow users to define engagement in their own terms, verify categories found in prior studies, examine the affective components of engagement, and represent engagement as a multi-dimensional construct.

Jacques' findings and approaches were built upon by O'Brien [154], who also conducted interviews for the purposes of examining the definition and key attributes of engagement. She employed semi-structured interviews that were informed by an interdisciplinary literature review and three frameworks: Play, Flow, and Aesthetic theories, which provided essential questions upon which to focus. Seventeen people who identified themselves as online searchers, gamers, learners, or shoppers were interviewed. O'Brien [154] used the critical incident technique [57] whereby interviewees were asked to think of a time in recent memory when they felt engaged while using the application they chose to discuss in the interview. The interviews were transcribed and analyzed qualitatively, and an independent inter-rater was used to examine the reliability of the codes and their application.

The outcomes of this analysis were two-fold. First of all, O'Brien confirmed and expanded upon previously identified attributes of engagement based on the works of [87] and [206]: challenge, aesthetic and sensory appeal, feedback, novelty, interactivity, control, perceived time, awareness, motivation, interest, and affect. Secondly, she put forward a process model of engagement with distinct stages of engaging with digital media (point of engagement), sustaining the engagement, disengaging, and re-engaging with the same or a different application within the same session or at another point in time. She mapped the engagement attributes to this process model, proposing that some attributes were more salient at different points in the process than others. In this study, the semi-structured interview enabled O'Brien to capture participants' engagement in their own words, to confirm the contributions of previous works regarding the attributes of engagement, and to model the process of user engagement in a visual and descriptive way.

2.4   THINK ALOUD AND THINK AFTER PROTOCOLS

Think aloud and think after (also known as stimulated recall) involve asking people to verbalize their thoughts and feelings during or after they perform a specific task, such as playing a video game or interacting with a museum exhibit.

2.4.1   THINK ALOUD

We typically consider think aloud as an exchange between researchers and participants, but this method may be used to elicit verbalizations from two or more people interacting with each other and a technology, such as a table top display. Thinking aloud may be allowed to occur spontaneously (i.e., when the participant wishes to verbalize) [54] or at fixed intervals (e.g., every three minutes) or points (e.g., when searchers reach a results page) during the interaction [96]. We can also distinguish between what people are being asked to do when they "think aloud:" describe what they are doing procedurally, or why they are performing specific actions.

In "Verbal Reports as Data," Ericsson & Simon refer to three levels of verbalization: vocalization; vocalization and verbal encoding; and verbalization with scanning or filtering and intermediate inference or generative processes [53]. Vocalization is the basic component of all three levels, and involves people verbalizing their thoughts or "inner speech" as they complete a task. The researcher may prompt the individual to continue to vocalize their thoughts if they fall silent. Verbal encoding occurs when the thought in the participant's mind is non-verbal in nature, such as an image, and he or she needs to offer more description about it to the researcher. Lastly, asking participants to scan or filter information from their environments, or report on their reasons or motives for completing behaviors that participants would not typically attend constitutes the final level of verbalization; this latter level interferes with people's focus on the primary task. This has been one of the main issues with think alouds, that people's cognitive processes are changed as a result of having to verbalize them [59], though Ericsson defended the method, saying it elicited "valid non-reactive reports of their thoughts" [52]. Another issue is that it is not possible to use time as a behavioral metric because the act of thinking aloud makes it an unreliable indicator of task performance.

Indeed, the scientific validity of introspective verbal reports was questioned in the first half of the 20th century [52], but much research has been conducted to defend their utility. Ericsson & Simon compared performance accuracy in participants who completed the same tasks either silently or while thinking aloud and reported no performance differences. They maintain "the closest connection between actual thoughts and verbal reports is found when people verbalize thoughts that are spontaneously attended during task completion" [52]. Yet, Van Den Haak et al. [200] claimed that think aloud did have a negative effect on task performance in their study. Krahmer & Ummelen [107] found that training participants to talk aloud did not affect their performance, but did lead to less disorientation in their navigation of websites. Lastly, Olmsted-Hawala et al. [156] compared a silent condition and three different modes of administering think alouds: the traditional Ericsson and Simon method with limited researcher interaction; speech-communication protocol with "back channels" (active listening, facial expressions, and body language) from the researcher; and coaching method where the test administrator actively probes participants' mental model of how something works. They concluded that those in the coaching condition were more successful and more satisfied.

2.4.2 THINK AFTER

The issue of reactivity or interference with cognitive process is one reason why some researchers adopt think after methods. If participants are asked to discuss an interaction after the fact, their attention will be less divided and cognitive load lessened than with think aloud methods [26]. However, one major issue common to other self-report methods is that this technique relies on people memories, which may be susceptible to "forgetting or fabrication." In addition, it can be difficult for participants to remember the details of complex tasks [26]. Nonetheless, in the case of HCI or IR tasks, researchers are able to draw participants' attention to specific features of an application or tool, or to replay the interaction using screen capture software to facilitate recall [96]. Recall is also improved when participants verbalize immediately following an event, rather than at a later time. Branch reasoned that think after allowed participants to be more reflective and insightful about their decision making process, in contrast to think aloud that only provided a narrative of what was occurring [26]. Frequently researchers record the interaction, e.g., log files, videos, screen captures. This secondary data can help participants with their recall; the researcher replays the on-screen interaction and asks the participant to respond to questions: "It looks like you are modifying your search terms here. What were you thinking at this point?"

2.4.3   RELATIONSHIP TO USER ENGAGEMENT

Few studies have been conducted using think aloud or think after to study user engagement. One example is O'Brien & Lebow's study of news browsers [149]. They asked participants to locate three items of their own choosing from a news website that would be suitable for sharing in a social situation. Of primary interest in this study was the relationship between social motivation and engagement. Morae[1] screen capture software was used to review the browsing session with participants. Participants were asked to pause on the articles they selected as part of the task scenario, and the researcher discussed with them their motivation for selecting the articles, how they would rate them in terms of interest, curiosity, and how willing they would be to share them in a social setting. Thus this study did not employ think after in its strictest sense because it asked semi-structured questions about the articles they chose and focused on specific points during the interaction. Nonetheless, asking participants to report their motivations for selecting news items revealed interesting insights about user engagement with content and news media.

2.5   QUESTIONNAIRES

Questionnaires are commonly used in HCI research, and user engagement research more specifically. They provide a convenient way to access users' perceptions of specific or general systems or experiences with technology; can be electronic, paper-based, or oral; can be administered to one person or groups of people; and can gather closed-ended (quantitative) or open-ended (qualitative) responses, depending on the exploratory nature of the research. Questionnaires are most effective when they are developed over time and with attention to instrument design, testing, and re-testing. Peterson delineates seven distinct steps in the construction of a questionnaire: review literature and requirements; develop and prioritize a list of questions or items; assess potential questions or items; determine types of questions to be asked; decide on specific wording; determine the structure of the questionnaire; and evaluate [164]. Table 2.1 outlines these steps and how they have been operationalized, as well as studies that have employed them.

Conducting longitudinal work to develop and evaluate a questionnaire for user engagement can be daunting. After all, technology changes rapidly, users' expectations rapidly increase, and designers of web, gaming, or mobile applications, e-learning portals, etc., need to measure the effects of their product in a timely manner. Yet failure to invest in the development and evaluation process results in poor measures and the perception that questionnaires are an unreliable and invalid way of measuring user engagement.

Yet even when questionnaires are well designed, they must be administered with the knowledge of limitations specific to questionnaires. These limitations are well documented in the physiology literature and thoroughly summarized by Kelly et al. [99]. In addition to inflation and acquiescence, which were addressed in a previous section, Kelly et al. relay that people may fail to elaborate adequately when answering open-ended questions, and that the amount of effort

---

[1]http://www.techsmith.com/morae.html.

Table 2.1: Steps in questionnaire construction derived from [164]

Steps in Questionnaire Construction	Operationalization	References
Review Literature and Requirements	Examine academic and trade press literature for definitions and dimensions of specific constructs, or global measures of the construct.	[7, 116, 150]
	Examine previously constructed and tested instruments.	[136, 151]
Develop and prioritize a list of questions and items	Gather potential items based on step 1 and/or interviews with users or experts.	[151]
	Ask users or experts to suggest adjectives that describe the construct.	[87, 116]
Assess face and content validity of potential questions or items	Screen questions by asking users to examine potential items against definitions of specific constructs.	[7]
	Use the Delphi method with several rounds of evaluation.	[136]
Determine types of questions to be asked	Open-ended versus closed ended verbal stimuli: Are you asking people to: compare (more or less); endorse (true or not true); state the frequency of an action (always or never); comment on the influence of something (a major or minor event, problem, etc.); rate the intensity of agreement or disagreement	[164]
Decide on specific wording	Brevity; relevance; free of ambiguity, i.e., no "double barreled" questions, unfamiliar terms; consider that modifiers such as "very," "quite," etc., and "could," "should," and "might" will have multiple interpretations	[62, 104]
Determine the structure of the questionnaire	Visual appearance of the questionnaire. If using a rating scale, must determine number of categories, labeling and type: semantic differential (hot $ cold), Likert (strongly disagree $ strongly agree), or staple (-5 $ +5)	[164]
Evaluate the questionnaire	Dimensionality: pertains to whether the questionnaire reflects a single construct or trait. Reliability: internal consistency and test-retest reliability Validity: internal and external Generalizability: utility of questionnaire in different research settings	[7, 116, 136, 151, 152]

required to interpret questions, recall and reflect upon their experiences or attitudes, and communicate responses to items may result in "satisficing," where responses do not accurately reflect what they know or feel about an experience. Since we often ask people to complete questionnaires at the end of a research study when people are fatigued, the placement of the questionnaire in the sequence of the experimental design may have unintended consequences on respondents' perceived levels of engagement. However, as discussed in Section 2.4, administering questionnaires mid-study can disrupt the "flow" of the human-computer interaction and result in negative ratings for user engagement due to the interruption rather than the actual experience.

Furthermore, Kelly et al.'s own study confirmed effects of mode on participant responses. They asked people in an information retrieval study to complete the same usability questionnaire in one of three modes: pen and paper, electronic, or orally as part of an interview. With regard to the open-ended questions, people were more verbose and expressed more ideas in the interview than the electronic and pen and paper modes; though the authors cautioned that more data did not equate to better data and that the time of the researcher to code qualitative data was not insignificant. Of greater concern was the difference in average ratings of the closed-ended questions: participants who completed the electronic questionnaire gave more positive ratings than those in the other two modes [99]. The inflation of ratings for the electronic questionnaire reinforces the general concerns about inflated responses for questionnaires, and underscores the need to examine internal and external validity in the context of studies that employ questionnaires.

Some of these effects may be minimized through the research design. We could, for example, keep studies briefer or allow participants to rest periodically during experiments to mitigate the degree of cognitive effort participants are expending. We could select modes of administering questionnaires that result in the least amount of inflation, or use other self-report, performance, or physiological measures to assess the degree of inflation. However, one of the best ways to mitigate measurement error and bias is to use questionnaires that have been shown to be reliable and valid [96].

In summary, questionnaire development and evaluation is a longitudinal process [116] that should be guided by informed decision-making, rigorous testing, and attention to reliability and validity. It is essential to be aware of the general drawbacks of questionnaires to acknowledge these limitations and attempt to minimize their effects. However, using and improving upon existing measures is the optimal way to construct good questionnaires. In the following sections, we outline three questionnaires developed to measure user engagement that can be built upon, and then describe other questionnaires related to user engagement that may be employed to investigate particular facets of user engagement.

2.6 QUESTIONNAIRES FOR MEASURING USER ENGAGEMENT

There are a number of questionnaires for measuring user engagement: Survey to Evaluate User Engagement [87]; User Engagement Questionnaire and Influences on User Engagement Questionnaire [206]; User Engagement Scale (UES) [151]; and eHealth engagement scale [119]. While, for instance, the questionnaires in [87] and [206] were developed in the context of educational multimedia, O'Brien & Toms [151] constructed and tested their measure with e-shoppers, and the eHealth engagement scale is specific to the eHealth domain. Nonetheless, there are several commonalities amongst the questionnaires in terms of the attributes of user engagement they each attempt to assess.

2.6.1 SURVEY TO EVALUATE ENGAGEMENT

Jacques [87] developed a 13-item questionnaire to measure user engagement that encompassed the following attributes: attention, perceived time, motivation, needs, control, attitudes. The survey to evaluate engagement (SEE) evolved out of multiple studies that involved interviews with participants to gauge their responses to television commercials, and experiments where participants were asked to interact with educational multimedia CD-ROMs. Using what participants said they "liked" and "disliked" about the ads and CD-ROMs and why, Jacques created the SEE and piloted it with general uses and software experts. The revised SEE used a five-point Likert scale to rate items. Furthermore, Jacques provided a scoring rubric whereby an individual's total engagement could be calculated and classified as high, medium-high, medium-low, and low; he also proposed that scores could be calculated for each attribute measured by the SEE in order to see which attributes were rated as highest and lowest by participants.

Unfortunately, the SEE was only published as a Ph.D. dissertation with limited visibility. However, Jacques' work represents a systematic approach to the study of user engagement with digital media and the SEE was the first instrument of its kind. It relied on both user and expert feedback, provided direction on administering and scoring the questionnaire, and offered design guidelines based on the attributes it conveyed.

2.6.2   ENGAGEMENT AND INFLUENCES ON QUESTIONNAIRE

Webster & Ho [206] distinguished between items to measure engagement (attention focus, curiosity, intrinsic interest, and overall engagement) and influences on engagement (challenge, feedback, control, and variety). They focused on the system as an influence on engagement, but indicated that the user's task, organizational context, or traits could be considered influences. Their 15-item questionnaire was used to investigate perceived user engagement with two different multimedia presentation systems (Authorware and Powerpoint) in the classroom; thus they were not examining users' assessments of directly interacting with a system, but rather listener engagement. Two similar presentations were constructed and delivered using the presentation software. In study one, Authorware was manipulated to be more challenging, provide more feedback and student control, and to contain more variety through the inclusion of sound and animation. Study two was similar to study one, but this time the lecture was delivered by the course instructor using two versions of Authorware (less engaging and more engaging). They found that the seven-item questionnaire used to measure user engagement was unidimensional, and that challenge, control, and variety as influences on engagement were positively associated with user engagement; feedback was related to engagement in study one but not study two. The more engaging version of Authorware was rated more engaging in both studies.

Chapman et al. [35] used questions from the questionnaires developed in [87] and [206] to examine user engagement with a multimedia training system. They conducted two studies in which university students were asked to interact with a computer-based training simulation in one of three formats: video; audio plus still images; and text-transcript plus still images. The questionnaire used to measure engagement, which contained seven items in study one and nine in study two, was internally consistent. Results indicated that the video condition was more engaging than the audio and text conditions; media richness was also higher in the video condition. Performance, as measured by recall and inference tests, was higher in the video condition in study one, but not significantly different across format conditions in study two.

Subsequently, Webster & Ahuja [205] used the seven-item engagement measure to explore the relationship between engagement and perceived disorientation (i.e., "I felt lost" and "It was difficult to find a page that I had previously viewed") with a technical writing website presented with simple, basic, and enhanced navigation structures. They found that engagement was significantly and negatively correlated with disorientation, and that there was a significant positive association between engagement and self-reported intentions to use the system again in the future and the number of correct answers participants achieved on a recall test. However, there was no relationship between engagement and time spent using the systems or Internet experience.

Chen et al. [36] built upon [205] work on user engagement and disorientation, manipulating the familiarity, navigational breadth, and media richness of an e-commerce website. They found that the familiar, broad-based navigation, and media rich versions of the website were more engaging and less disorienting, and that people were more likely to want to use them in the future. They confirmed the relationship amongst these outcome variables using structural equation modeling: perceived disorientation negatively predicted future intention to use and engagement, while engagement positively influenced future intention to use. A significant conclusion reached by the authors was that these three variables are "synergistic rather than additive. This implies that one or more factors can compensate for the weakness of other factors." Thus Chen et al. used various self-report measures, including Webster & Ho's engagement questionnaire [206], to examine the relationship amongst various predictors and outcomes of web interactions, and provide some direction for engaging design based on manipulating the familiarity, richness, and navigational structure of a specific website.

Overall, the work of Webster and colleagues contributed a measure of user engagement that was successfully employed in studies of multimedia interactions. It utilized controlled experimental studies and established an agenda for future theoretical, methodological, and design work in user engagement.

2.6.3   USER ENGAGEMENT SCALE

The User Engagement Scale (UES) [151] is the newest questionnaire designed to measure user engagement and consists of 31 items and six sub-scales (aesthetic appeal, novelty, felt involvement, focused attention, perceived usability, and endurability or overall experience).

A comprehensive review of user engagement across multiple disciplines and interviews with technology users articulated proposed attributes of user engagement: challenge, positive affect, endurability, aesthetic and sensory appeal, attention, feedback, variety/novelty, interactivity, and perceived user control [150]. This led to the development of questionnaire items, which were derived from the interviews and existing measures for the attributes. Through screening, the list of potential items were assessed by an independent researcher for their correspondence to definitions for each of the attributes and pre-tested with a group of users for face validity and to address issues of wording and clarity. The resulting 123 items were administered to a sample of online shoppers. Exploratory factor analysis reduced redundancies amongst the items and clustered items into six underlying factors: aesthetic appeal, usability, focused attention, felt involvement, novelty, and endurability. A second online study was conducted with online shoppers of a specific retailer. The thirty-three item questionnaire with six sub-scales that resulted from the first study was administered. Structural equation modeling was used to confirm the factors and examine their relationship to each other. This resulted in a 31-item questionnaire.

The UES has been administered in studies with different types of technologies: an archival webcast system [153], a wikiSearch system [152], Facebook [18], and e-shopping [148]. These applications of the UES are compared in [152]. Firstly, each application of the 31-item UES has used factor or principle components analysis resulting in some items being eliminated during the process. For example, O'Brien & Toms's analysis retained 19 items [153], while their 2013 study resulted in 28 and Banhawi & Mohamed Ali's in 26 items [18]. The authors speculated that some items may be more salient for some applications (e-shopping versus information searching) or the setting in which they were administered (voluntarily using Facebook versus using an unfamiliar tool in an experimental setting). Secondly, some of the sub-scales were more stable than others. Usability, focused attention, and aesthetics consistently emerge as distinct factors across various studies. In three studies, novelty, felt involvement, and endurability merged to form one factor [18, 148, 152], while in another study the novelty and endurability sub-scales were stable, but the felt involvement items were eliminated during the analysis [153]. Based on these findings, the researchers suggested future improvements to the UES to ensure that the items for endurability, novelty, and felt involvement accurately reinforced these concepts, and that the questionnaire as a whole more clearly delineates between engagement with the task, system, and content [152].

The UES has been used in various studies to look at the relationship between user engagement and other variables of interest. These include studies using a simulated travel agency website [83], a haptic interface [123], and a crowdsourcing study on visual saliency [134].

Hyder [83] used components of the UES to explore engagement with a simulated online travel agency. Endurability items were included as measures of overall "value," aesthetic appeal usability items were part of the "antecedents of engagement," and focused attention and novelty items were used to measure curiosity. The selected items were examined with other performance and physiological measures to verify a model of user engagement with the website.

Levesque et al. [123] selected 10 items representing each of the aesthetic appeal, novelty, focused attention, usability, felt involvement, and endurability sub-scales to test users' interactions with four widgets presented on a touch-sensitive display surface that provided tactile feedback. They concluded that the selected UES items enabled them to compare users' engagement according to the level of tactile feedback afforded by the interface.

McCay-Peet et al. [134] used Amazon Mechanical Turk (a crowd-sourcing platform) to investigate how the visual saliency or catchiness of news headlines impacts aspects of user engagement, namely focused attention and affect. Among the measures they collected was the Positive and Negative Affect Schedule (PANAS) [204], focused attention (derived from the UES), and interest in the topics of the webpages with which they were asked to interact. Altering the display of information on the page, e.g., increasing or decreasing the font size of a headline manipulated saliency. Participants were then asked to perform eight information-seeking tasks using static webpages to locate the latest news or a headline on a specified entertainment topic. They found that when headlines/information were more visually salient, participants located task information quicker, maintained positive affect (based on pre- and post-task comparisons), and reported higher levels of focused attention. However, although users reported it was easier to focus in the salient condition, there were no significant differences between the UES focused attention items or perceived time on task across the salient and non-salient conditions. The authors speculated that this may have been because the study involved interactions with static webpages, which were necessary to control for saliency, rather than dynamic websites, and that the UES focused attention items may have been too abstract:

> "Examining saliency and engagement simultaneously in this study was a challenge. Salient features of a webpage draw user attention within the first few seconds of visiting a page, but engagement happens after, sometimes long after, that initial exposure."

UES has been used together with other measurement approaches (such as eye tracking and mouse tracking); we discuss these works in Chapter 6.

In summary, applications of the UES have had mixed results. Some of the studies demonstrated that items factored consistently for some of the sub-scales [18, 153], correlated well with other scales and produced similar predictive relationships [83], and were useful for capturing user engagement with haptic devices [123]. However, other studies [148, 152] have resulted in four factors or components rather than six, where novelty, felt involvement, and endurability items merge to form one factor/component. Furthermore, McCay-Peet et al. [134] did not detect significant differences in focused attention as measured by the UES in their study, but did find a relationship between saliency and focused attention in their open-ended question about the ease in which participants were able to focus on their task during the experiment. While this may have been due to the nature of interaction (static webpages), or perceptions of task versus experience, it may also have been due to response inflation [96].

2.6.4   eHEALTH ENGAGEMENT SCALE

Lefebvre et al. [119] developed a domain specific measure, the eHealth Engagement Scale based on research in the field of television advertising. They identified four attributes from prior research: involving, credible, negative feelings, and amusing/friendly, and examined these in an experiment that used static webpages representing nine health content areas. Participants were asked to examine the webpages using one of three scenarios: looking for information for someone they knew; determining if they or someone they knew had a health problem based on the information presented; and seeking information for the purposes of preventing health issues. Using structural equation modeling, they found that content perceived to be involving (absorbing, attention-grabbing, stimulating, and surprising); credible (convincing, balanced, believable); not dull; and cool/hip predicted users' feelings of confidence in the information they examined and their intention to act in general and within the next month more specifically. They also found that self-reported engagement varied according to content (health topic), delivery (webpage presentation), and individual differences, namely socio-demographic groups. They concluded that the eHealth Engagement Scale was a useful tool for measuring user engagement in the eHealth context, where the emphasis is on motivation and health behavior change.

2.7   CONSTRUCTS RELATED TO USER ENGAGEMENT

Studies on user engagement have examined a variety of other constructs in addition to or instead of engagement. Although these constructs may be measured with several different methods, here the focus is on self-report methods.

2.7.1   MENTAL WORKLOAD

Longo [125] proposed that mental workload indices, in conjunction with log data, could be used to measure cognitive engagement. Mental workload refers to the relationship between the cognitive resources available to engage in a task, compared to those required to do a task. Examples of self-report measures of mental workload are NASA Task Load Index (TLX), Subjective Workload Assessment Technique (SWAT), and Workload Profile (WP). The NASA TLX consists of seven dimensions: mental demands, physical demands, temporal demands, performance, effort, and frustration. Each of these is rated on a scale with 21 gradations ranging from very low to very high and a weighted rating score is calculated [73]. SWAT looks at workload according to three dimensions: time load, mental effort load, and physiological stress, and asks people to rate these dimensions as low, medium, or high within a particular context [171]. Lastly, the WP asks users to rate the attention they allocated to a task according to eight dimensions: perceptual/central processing, response selection and execution, spatial, processing, verbal processing, visual processing, auditory processing, manual output, and speech output [199]. Rubio et al. [178] provide an overview of NASA TLX, SWAT, and WP and their physiological properties. Based on two experiments, they provide guidance on the use of these measures depending on whether the goal is to predict individual performance, compare the difficulty of two or more tasks, or assess the degree of cognitive demand or attention required to complete a task.

Regardless of which self-report measure of mental workload is employed, there is undoubtedly a relationship between engagement and workload. We might hypothesize that feeling time pressure, stressed, overwhelmed, etc., during a human-computer interaction negates the possibility of engagement. However, appropriate levels of challenge have been noted as an important quality of engagement [150, 206], so we might speculate that low cognitive load might be as disengaging as high mental workload. Thus for mental workload to be used as a proxy for user engagement, more effort should be made to understand the relationship between the two constructs.

2.7.2   DISORIENTATION

Given the strong negative correlation between user engagement and disorientation [205], perceived disorientation is an effective means of assessing the engagement potential of systems. Perceived disorientation is "the tendency to lose one's sense of location and direction in a non-linear document" [205]. Webster & Ahuja [205] found that there was a negative relationship between users' perceptions of website disorientation and engagement, and that engagement was an important predictor of future intention to use the system and performance. The authors noted that they experimented with a formal information retrieval system, and that similar findings may not be obtained for exploratory search systems. However, if interested in information retrieval and web search systems, [7] the seven-item disorientation questionnaire may be a useful measure, since high degrees of disorientation will be associated with low levels of engagement, and vice versa. Thus, disorientation may be used not only to gauge the navigational ease of websites, but also to validate measures of user engagement.

2.7.3   PLAYFULNESS

Play is the physical activity that encourages learning and creativity, develops and satisfies psychological and social needs, and involves aspects of competition and collaboration [174]. Play has been associated with having user experiences, such as news reading [190] and browsing [197], and has also been examined in the context of educational technologies [174, 181], video games [162], and decision making on the web [14]. Play is linked with increased frequency and satisfaction of system use, and has been attributed to increased motivation, challenge, and affect [209]. Thus elements of play are intrinsic to engagement, and may manifest in the interactivity of the application.

Play theory has been used to ground user engagement. O'Brien & Toms [150], for example, speculated that some of the characteristics of play (aesthetic appeal, affective appeal, challenge, feedback, goal-directedness, motivation, and sensory appeal), may be essential attributes of user engagement. Webster & Martocchio [207] defined microcomputer playfulness as "a situation-specific individual characteristic [that] represents a type of intellectual or cognitive playfulness. It describes an individual's tendency to interact spontaneously, inventively, and imaginatively with microcomputers." They created a measure of microcomputer playfulness and evaluated its reliability and validity in two training sessions and three survey studies with university students. They focused specifically on the state of playfulness rather than the trait, distinguishing between situation-specific experiences and stable individual traits. In addition to assessing the physiological properties of the microcomputer playfulness scale, they found positive relationships between playfulness and attitudes toward computers, perceived competency with computers, and computer self-efficacy. They also found that playfulness predicted user satisfaction, involvement, positive affect, and learning.

The relationship between playfulness and engagement could be explored in more depth, though we could hypothesize that engaging systems will share some of the characteristics of playful systems, and lead to similar outcomes of satisfaction, learning, etc. Playfulness could also be used to determine why users find one system more engaging than another.

2.7.4 COGNITIVE ABSORPTION

Another highly relevant construct is cognitive absorption (CA) [13]. Argawal & Karahanna [13] describe the origins of cognitive absorption (CA) as being rooted in Tellegen's psychological trait of absorption, Flow Theory [44], and cognitive engagement [206]. They developed and tested a self-report measure based on five dimensions of CA: temporal dissociation, focused immersion, heightened enjoyment, control, and curiosity. They found that CA predicted perceived use and ease of use of information systems, and that it was influenced by microcomputer playfulness and personal innovativeness. Given the number of shared attributes between user engagement and CA (i.e., focused attention, positive affect, novelty/curiosity, etc.), the CA scale may be used to validate measures of user engagement, or to focus on specific dimensions of engagement, such as focused attention.

2.8 SUMMARY

This chapter described self-report methods, specifically interviews, think aloud/think after protocols, and questionnaires, and provided some examples of how these methods are being used to study engagement. In general, many studies have followed a trajectory of using interviews to define engagement and its attributes, and moved into developing questionnaires or conducting experiments with various technologies and techniques once they felt they had a better grasp of the construct. The studies described here show a mixture of free response, discrete, and dimensional approaches to the study of user engagement. In addition, we have included related self-report measures that may be useful for understanding the relationship between individual traits or states and user engagement, and for bolstering the validity of other measures employed in the study of user engagement.

A fundamental issue in the selection of self-report methods is the research question, the setting (field or laboratory) and the degree of structure and control to be included in the research design. Each method, as discussed here, has its opportunities and drawbacks that must be weighed in employing it in a study. However, selecting the most appropriate measure and implementing it correctly can address some of the limitations of self-report. Overall, self-report methods may be used to gather data explicitly about engagement, or to predict, validate, or enrich other measures of engagement.

CHAPTER 3

Approaches Based on Physiological Measurements

Physiological measures assess how the body functions. They may be simple, e.g., measuring body temperature with a thermometer, or more complicated, e.g., measuring heart function using an electrocardiograph [8]. Physiological measures of interest to us are those related to cognitive or affective states that can be captured by sensors, cameras, or software. These include measures gathered through:

- Eye tracking, where measures such as pupil dilation and fixation have been used as indicators of task difficulty, attention, fatigue, mental activity, and intense emotion;

- Mouse pressure, which has been associated with stress, or certainty of response; and

- Biosensors, including temperature (used to assess negative affect and relaxation), electrodermal activity (associated with arousal), blood flow (used as an indicator of stress and emotion intensity); and muscle movement or facial expression (associated with emotional response and attention).

Many of these measures have been shown to relate to attention, affect, aesthetics, and/or novelty in various works, and as such, have the potential to be highly indicative of engagement. For instance, Jennett et al. [89] used eye tracking data to assess immersion, and found that eye movement increased over time during a non-immersed experience, but reduced over time during an immersed experience. In other words, users seem to focus on fewer targets during engaged attention.

We start by describing a subset of physiological measures, referred to as psychophysiological measures, which include measures of bodily and brain response and functioning. We then discuss the use of eye tracking, mouse (cursor) tracking and cameras for recording user behavior. A large part of this chapter is dedicated to eye tracking and cursor tracking, because of their extensive investigations as measurement tools and potential (in particular mouse tracking) in the study of user engagement.

We are interested in the usage of physiological measures to assess "everyday" types of engagement such as reading news and spending time on social networking sites, but not on extreme behaviors (such as immersion in games) or those associated with medical conditions. For these, the conference[1] on "Approaches to Causality in Engagement, Immersion and Presence on Performance and Human-Computer Interaction" contains many relevant works and references.

3.1   PSYCHOPHYSIOLOGICAL MEASUREMENTS

Psychophysiology is the branch of physiology dealing with the relationship between physiological processes and thoughts, emotions, and behavior [55]. The body responds to psychological processes. For example, when we get nervous, we sweat; when we get embarrassed, our cheeks get red and warm. These types of mind and body relationships started to be explored early in the 20th century. However, psychophysiology did not emerge as a separate sub-discipline until the mid 20th. In addition, physiology has usually explored the effects of physiological changes, in particular neurophysiological ones, on behavioral and mental outcome measures, and typically conducted animal experiments, whereas psychophysiology explored the effects of psychological changes on physiological outcome measures, typically through experiments carried out on humans. Nowadays, the distinction between psychophysiology and physiology is mostly blurred, and both are subsumed within neuroscience more generally.

Psychophysiology may be captured using instruments, such as sensors, or measures, such as pupil aperture. The following list includes a combination of these types and is meant to provide a broad picture of the type of psychophysiological data that can be gathered, how it is gathered, and what it indicates with respect to human cognitive or affective states.

- *Electroencephalogram (EEG)*: EEG records the electrical activity along the scalp, produced by the firing of neurons. EEG measures rhythmic activity, defined according to a frequency range. Rhythmic activity within a certain frequency range was noted to have a certain distribution over the scalp and leading to a certain biological significance. EEG has successfully been used to discern between different affective states.

- *Functional magnetic resonance imaging (fMRI)*: This measures the brain activity by detecting associated changes in blood flow. When an area of the brain is in use, blood flow to that region increases. fMRI has been used in the context of search, showing differences in the brain activity depending on whether the user was dealing with relevant versus non-relevant information.

- *Cardiovascular measures*: These include heart rate (HR), beats per minute (BPM), heart rate variability (HRV), and inter-beat interval (IBI). When the heart functions normally, each IBI value (measured in milliseconds) varies from beat to beat. This natural variation is known as HRV. Some cardiac conditions may cause the IBI values to become nearly constant, resulting in the HRV being nearly zero. This can happen during periods of exercise as the heart rate increases and the beats become regular. Several studies showed that cardiac activity correlates with affective states.

---

[1]http://www.inputs-outputs.org.

- *Respiratory sensors*: These monitor oxygen intake and carbon dioxide output. The measurement is similar to heart rate rhythms: the average respiration period which is defined as the time duration of a single breath cycle can vary according to emotional states.

- *Electromyographic (EMG) sensors*: EMG measures the electrical activity produced by skeletal muscles, some of which are shown to strongly correlate with affective states.

- *Pupillometry*: This measures variations in the diameter of the pupillary aperture of the eye in response to stimuli. For instance, the pupil may dilate due to an increase of the light or because of mental or emotional reasons.

- *Skin Conductance Level (SCL)*: This measures perspiration/sweat gland activity. SCL measures the electrical conductance of the skin, which varies in presence or absence of sweat. The SCL values increase when the sweating glands, controlled by the autonomous nervous system, release more sweat because of motor or mental increased activity. This measure has been shown to correlate with affective phenomena.

- *Temperature sensors*: These measure changes in blood flow and body temperature.

A recent work explored some of the above measures to study user engagement in the context of a widely used social network site, Facebook [131]. Mauri et al. explored whether Facebook elicited a specific psychophysiological pattern by recording skin conductance level (SCL) and electrical muscle activity (EMG). These are known to relate to the valence and arousal model of Lang's theory of emotion [113]. More specifically, the SCL values are distributed along the Y-axis, representing the dimension of arousal, from low arousal to high arousal; whereas the EMG values are distributed along the X-axis, representing the dimension of valence, from positive to negative valence.

Thirty subjects were exposed to a slide show of natural panoramas (relaxation condition), then to the subject's personal Facebook account, and finally to a mathematical task (stress condition); each of these exposures was for 3 minutes in duration. According to the Arousal-Valence model, the Facebook exposure fell in the upper left quadrant of the affective space, which is associated with an affective state defined by moderate to high degrees of both dimensions, i.e., enjoyable and exciting experience. The authors also measured pupil dilation, and found that the Facebook exposure was significantly different from stress and relaxation.

These findings support the hypothesis that the successful spread of Facebook may be associated with a specific positive affective state experienced by users when they use it. Important for our understanding on how to measure engagement, neither the subjects (university students in this case) nor the experiences were "extreme." However, the experiences were sufficiently different. Whether the same could be observed with a standard news reading experience across sites is something that needs to be investigated.

In the context of search, Moshfeghi et al. [139] investigated the connection between relevance and brain activity. The brain activity of eighteen participants was measured using fMRI as they were tasked to assess the relevance of known relevant and non-relevant images for given queries. They identified three brain regions in the frontal, parietal, and temporal cortex where brain activity differed when processing relevant and non-relevant images. This study brings new insights toward a better understanding of the concept of relevance, which has been the subject of numerous works in information retrieval (e.g., [137]). How to operationalize these insights into effective retrieval algorithms remains to be tackled.

Psychophysiology measurement can assist in the understanding of user engagement and other phenomena. They have several advantages over both self-report measurements (for example via questionnaires) or online behavior analytics, since they are more directly connected to the emotional state of the user, are more objective (involuntary body responses) and they are continuously measured. However, to be able to measure engagement for average users and their experiences, we may need to conduct "large-scale" studies to obtain significant insights. How large a study is in itself an interesting and important question to ask, and one to consider when exploring these types of measures, as they continue to be expensive to conduct, cumbersome, and obtrusive. Finally, more research is required to refine our understanding of precisely what physiological states are indicative of engagement and how to differentiate against negative states of high arousal such as stress.

3.2   FACIAL EXPRESSIONS

In the context of search, implicit feedbacks (e.g., click on a search result, dwell time on a result page, skip on the search result page) have been to shown to be effective indicators of document relevance or non-relevance. Ranking algorithms that incorporate these signals have led to considerable improvement in search effectiveness. Arapakis et al. [10] looked at an additional implicit feedback signal, facial expression, in presence of relevant versus non-relevant results. A facial expression is one or more motions or positions of the facial muscles. These movements (motions and positions) often convey the emotional state of a person. There are many tools that can detect users' facial expression when interacting with a computer or an interface. These tools are able to perform real-time, frame-by-frame analysis of the emotional responses of users, detecting and tracking expressions of primary emotions, for instance, joy, surprise, anger, disgust, sadness, and fear, but also more advanced emotions, such as frustration and confusion.

In their work, Arapakis et al. [10] recorded the facial expressions of 16 subjects, while performing search tasks of various levels of difficultly. They then extracted a set of features from the facial expression data, which they then classified using a machine learning approach. They showed that incorporating these lead to a noticeable improvement in the performance of a model to predict relevance. Overall, this work demonstrates that facial expressions provide good cues on topical relevance. Although extracting these features for a whole population of users, for example, using a particular search engine, is not likely possible, such approaches can help in assessment and labeling tasks, which are performed in large quantities in the context of search engine evaluation.

How this work can extend to other areas than search and other engagement factors than relevance remains to investigated.

3.3 EYE TRACKING

Eye tracking is the process of measuring either the point of gaze, i.e., where one is looking, the motion of an eye relative to the head, or changes in pupil dilation. An eye tracker is a device measuring eye positions and movements, and pupillometry. Here we focus on eye positions and movements. The most popular method for measuring these uses video images from which the eye position is extracted. Table 3.1 lists some metrics that can be extracted to measure eye movement and position (these were used in [95]). These metrics can be calculated for the whole screen or with respect to defined so-called Areas of Interest (AOIs). In the context of a news experience, typical AOIs include title of a news article, its first paragraph or the whole article body. In the context of search, AOIs may include the query box, the main panel displaying the organic results and any of the segments listing the sponsored search results.

Table 3.1: Example of eye metrics used to analyze gaze behavior (from [95])

Time to First Fixation: Time taken (in seconds) before a participant fixates (on an AOI) for the first time.
Fixations Before: Number of times a participant fixates on the media before fixating (on an AOI) for the first time.
First Fixation Duration: Duration of the first fixation (on an AOI).
Fixation Duration: Duration of each individual fixation (within an AOI).
Total Fixation Duration: Sum of the duration for all fixations (within an AOI).
Fixation Count: Number of times a participant fixates (on an AOI).
Visit Duration: Duration of each individual visit (within an AOI).
Visit Count: Number of visits (within an AOI).

Gaze has been considered an indicator of attention focus. When we read, examine a scene, or search for an object, we continuously make eye movements, which are called saccades. More precisely, saccades are rapid movements that occur when we change focus. When the visual gaze is maintained on a single location for several milliseconds we have a fixation. An eye tracker used in many studies, including [11], is the Tobii 1750 eye tracker,[2] which is integrated into a monitor. When activated, the eye tracker illuminates the user with two infrared projections that generate reflection patterns on the corneas of the eyes. A video camera gathers these reflection patterns along with the position of the user and, through digital image processing, the pupil locations are extracted. The pupil positions are then mapped to gaze locations on the screen [11].

Eye tracking provides fine-grained data and resolution that allows us to directly measure what users are looking at. This has allowed us to obtain numerous insights into how people consume and browse webpages, for example the famous "F" shape of how users read web content.[3]

---

[2]http://www.tobii.com.
[3]http://www.nngroup.com/articles/f-shaped-pattern-reading-web-content/.

The relationship between attention, an important component of user engagement, and eye movements has been investigated extensively in various works [56, 169, 172, 185]. Gaze behavior has also been studied in information processing tasks like reading [30], visual search [161], scene perception [75], and in micro-blogging [43]. As stated in [11], the "importance of gaze in the assessment of engagement lies in the fact that, although looking might appear to be a process that is under voluntary control, conscious and deliberate control of fixation happens infrequently. As with other components of voluntary performance (e.g., walking or maintenance of balance), looking is controlled by a general intention, and consciousness plays a minor role in the execution of the intended sequence of fixations." We discuss some specific works related to user engagement in the rest of this section.

3.3.1   EYE TRACKING AND SEARCH

In the context of search, Buscher et al. [31] determined which parts of a document was read, skimmed, or skipped by interpreting eye movements. When associating read and skimmed parts as relevant, and ignoring skipped document parts, retrieval performance (mostly re-ranking the results) were shown to considerably improve. They also reported considerable improvements when using gaze-based feedback on the segment level (which part of the document was read or nor read) compared to relevance feedback on the document level (stating that a document was relevant or not).

In a separate study, Buscher et al. [32] examined how users interact with organic versus sponsored search. The type of task (informational or navigational), the quality of the ads (relevant or irrelevant to the query), and the sequence in which ads of different quality were presented varied. They found that the amount of visual attention that people devote to organic results depends on both task type and ad quality. The amount of visual attention that people devote to ads depends on their quality, but not the type of task. Finally, the sequence and predictability of ad quality was found to be an important factor in determining how much people attend to ads. When the quality of ads varied randomly from task to task, people paid little attention to the ads, even when they were good. These results show how attention devoted to search results is influenced by other page elements, and how previous search experiences influence how people attend to the current page. These results are important to understand how users engage with various components of their search, and their likely behavior in their future engagement (for instance ignoring ads).

3.3.2   EYE TRACKING AND READING

In the context of a news reading experience, Arapakis et al. [11] quantified the effect of user interest on attention, by examining gaze behavior. They observed how eye metrics like "Total Fixation Duration," "Fixation Count," and "Visit Count" (see Table 3.1), differed across online news of varying levels of interestingness. They found that participants spend significantly more time browsing the titles of interesting articles, performed more gaze visits, as well as quicker to occur, more frequent, and prolonged fixations.

The authors also examined the association of gaze behavior and sentiment.[4] Their analysis revealed that longer and more frequent fixations occurred when users were viewing news titles characterized by low sentimentality and positive polarity. In the context of predicting user engagement, this suggests that gaze behavior can act as a proxy for sentiment, and more importantly, vice versa. In other words, gaze behavior is measurable and can be anticipated to a certain degree by the writing style—in terms of sentimentality—of the news articles. The importance of this cannot be underestimated. Indeed, understanding what happens when the user is exposed to new information is crucial, as it is during this attention process that the user decides whether the content is worth reading or not [11].

3.3.3 EYE TRACKING AND SELECTION

Selecting one among several items in a visual display is a common task: which news item to read or which product item to explore. Visual attention is in many contexts part of the selection process, and deciphering this process requires understanding what draws visual attention, what sustains it, and how these factors influence the selection. This problem is challenging as the process involves a wide range of factors—from low-level visual factors, such as visual saliency and the position of items, to high-level semantic factors, such as the user's interests or preferences for various items.

To provide some insights about the above, Navalpakkam et al. [144] performed a study to investigate the relative importance of position, saliency, and user interest in drawing and sustaining attention in multi-item selection tasks and how any of these factors affect the task of selection. They carried out a study where users were asked to select one of eight news items they would read. The eye movements of the users were recorded while they performed the selection. The saliency (with respect to the images shown with the articles) and the position of the news items were varied, and users were also asked to rate afterward if they found the selected news items interesting.

The authors found that attention shifts were dominated by visual factors such as position and saliency. They also found that position played a dominant role, with significantly more time spent at top-left positions than other positions. This aligns with eye tracking studies that revealed the so-called "golden triangle heatmap" (in the Western world) [78], which is an attention bias toward the top-left positions in a display. However, they then found that the final selection depended mainly on user interest, followed by position, and attention—specifically how long the user attends to an item, but not how quickly they attend to it. This clearly show that users' interest is what primarily drives the user to select which article to read, and that position and where the user focuses on are secondary. "Interesting content comes first."

---

[4]To compute the degree (sentimentality) and sign (polarity) of the sentiments expressed in the news articles they used SentiStrength, a widely used lexicon-based, sentiment analysis tool [195].

3.3.4 SUMMARY AND LIMITATIONS

Eye tracking has led to numerous insights regarding how users engage with websites; we discussed several in the above section. The usage of eye tracking in the context of measuring user engagement has been mainly on visual focus and attention (i.e., what attracts users' gaze). However, what interests users, for example, in terms of selecting which news items to consume, has also been shown to relate to measures of eye movement. In Chapter 6, we discuss how eye movements has been shown to correlate with other engagement criteria, such as focus attention and positive affect (measured through self-report methods).

Eye tracking, however, has some limitations. Studies that use eye tracking methods are not scalable because we need people to come and sit in front of the eye tracker. However, this may be changing. Lagun & Agichtein [111] proposed a way to simulate eye tracking–based measurement in the context of web search. Eye trackers are also expensive, making their use limited to those who have access to usability laboratories and equipment. Eye tracking glasses, which are now becoming commercially available, may however change this in the near future, e.g., [160].

As previously stated, using eye tracking means that, in most cases, users must come to the place where the experiment is being carried out, which is not a natural environment for the participant (like home or work), and users will behave differently in a laboratory setting. This is particularly an issue when measuring user engagement, as engagement is not a one-session "thing" but a relationship "thing" between the user and the technology. This is why another type of physiological measurement, one based on cursor tracking, has great potential. The ability of mouse movements to act as a proxy of gaze is discussed in the next section.

3.4 CURSOR TRACKING

Many characteristics of user engagement are difficult to measure on a large scale, for instance, interestingness, aesthetics, and novelty. However, it may be possible for this information to be gathered through an analysis of cursor data. Mouse tracking (also known as cursor tracking) is the use of software (for example written in JavaScript) to collect users' mouse cursor positions on the computer. Examples of mouse movements include: number of coordinates, total distance traveled (along the x- and y-axis), movement speed, and any minimal or maximal coordinates. Scroll movements can be accounted for in their frequency and their speed. Predefined areas of interests (AOIs) can be defined, in the same manner as for eye tracking. Edmonds et al. [49] argued for measuring engagement using tools such as cursor tracking, noting that there is considerable work correlating eye movement and gaze [37, 79].

Studying fine-grained interactions such as mouse cursor movements [67, 79, 175] is an active area of research, with a strong focus on search, as these interactions provide additional insights into searcher behavior compared to coarser models of clicks alone. In particular, recent work has demonstrated the coordination between the gaze movements and the cursor movements [68, 79, 175] and showed that both gaze and cursor interactions are informative of user attention [45, 67] and preferences [69, 81]. Search engine companies have also investigated and modeled the cursor data to improve understanding of result examination patterns [175], ranking of search results [5], understanding of search result abandonment (a search session with no clicks) [81], and evaluation of content layout and noticeability [142]. We discuss some of these works, with a particular focus on how they can inform us about measuring user engagement.

3.4.1   ALIGNING EYE GAZE AND MOUSE MOVEMENT

We start with work analyzing how eye gaze and cursor movement align outside the search domain, then focus on work carried out in search.

Aligning Eye Gaze and Mouse Movement Outside Search

Navalpakkam & Churchill [142] studied how mouse and gaze align when users read several articles from a news (finance) website, all of them with rich media content. They were three scenarios: putting some ads at the top of the article, at the top right of the article, and at random positions in the article. Each user was associated with one of these scenarios. The aim was to study whether mouse and gaze align or not, depending on where the ads were positioned. Overall, the patterns for each were similar. There was a shift in attention (gaze and mouse) from top-left to right as the position of the ad changed. There was stronger attention at the top of the page, and longer dwell time on the left of the page. Finally, the fixed ads—position wise—were visited sooner while more time was needed to process when the position of the ads changed. The experiment brought interesting insights into the ad avoidance phenomenon; but overall, this study suggests that there are similar patterns between gaze and mouse in terms of user attention.

Chen et al. [37] studied the relationship between gaze position and cursor position of users browsing several websites. They found a strong relationship between gaze position and cursor position and observed regular patterns of eye/mouse movements. For instance, the dwell time of cursor among different regions of a webpage had a strong correlation to how likely a user will look at that region. This means that in terms of predicting users' interests on webpages, mouse movement is a good alternative to an eye tracker.

The relationship between eye gaze and mouse cursor movements was also studied in a debugging task by Chen & Lim [38]. Debugging difficulty was manipulated (there were three error types: lexical, logical, and syntactic) to measure the effects on debugging performance (accuracy and reaction time) on eye gaze and mouse cursor behavior. Mouse cursor behavior was a significant indication of the level of difficulty and therefore debugging performance. The general pattern of mouse movements was comparable with eye gaze patterns, but also the mouse data led to additional insights from eye gaze (the level of difficulty could be better predicted when accounting for both). This work supports the idea of using mouse tracking to infer intentions and other characteristics of user engagement.

Aligning Eye Gaze and Mouse Movement in Search

The bulk of work relating gaze and mouse movement is found in the context of web search, where engagement here is with respect to the user's interests in the results (their relevance) returned by a search engine. The relationship between eye and mouse movements have been explored both in laboratory studies and at scale. Rodden et al. [175] measured the eye and mouse movements of 32 users performing search tasks in a laboratory setting. They identified multiple patterns of eye-mouse coordination: the mouse following the eye in the x and y directions, marking a result, and remaining stationary. Moreover, the mouse sometimes was shown to lead the eye horizontally (this was however not very common), to follow the eye vertically (this was very common), and too often be stationed at position likely indicating a result being carefully examined. Incidental mouse usage was also identified, where the mouse was used for clicking somewhere on the page or manipulating the web browser, where it was found to be less correlated with eye gaze. Overall Rodden et al. and other works e.g., [68, 81] demonstrate that the correlation on search result pages is higher along the y-axis than x-axis, and is stronger when the cursor is placed over relevant or interesting search results.

A study by Huang et al. [79], who looked into this relationship further, identified several factors affecting how gaze and mouse align. They found that eye-mouse distances peaked around 600 ms after a page loaded and decreased over time, and that the mouse tended to lag behind gaze by 700 ms on average. They classified cursor behaviors into the four patterns—Inactive, Examining (cursor moving but no reading or action), Reading, and Action (e.g., click on link, edit query, drag scrollbar)—and measured sizeable differences in mouse cursor position and gaze depending on the patterns. Overall, alignment between mouse cursor and gaze increased from "Inactive" to "Action."

Understanding how users examine a page with a nonlinear layout, such as informational panel to the right of the search results (e.g., the Knowledge Graph in Google), was carried out by Navalpakkam et al. [143]. They showed that using eye and mouse data, user attention on nonlinear page layouts was different from the typical top-down linear examination order of search results. They further demonstrated that the mouse, like the eye, is sensitive to two key page elements—position (layout), and their relevance to the user information need. Finally, they identified mouse measures that strongly correlated with eye movements. Again, this work showed that mouse tracking can be used to infer user attention, even for complex search result page layouts.

Recently, Lagun & Agichtein [111] proposed a method to perform remote eye tracking at large scale using mouse tracking. The search snippet was highlighted at the current mouse position and the rest of the search result page was blurred. By controlling the page visibility this way, they were able to measure the amount of attention devoted to the different search snippets as a function of their position on the page, and search relevance. They showed that it was possible to measure how long users dwell on a page element given that they notice it. However, this method cannot tell whether users actually notice the page element, which restricts its applicability as "noticing versus not noticing" is an important factor in the user selection process (e.g., which article to chose to read).

To conclude, many researchers have argued that cursor tracking data can provide a new way to learn about website visitors [49, 79]. Existing work shows that cursor movements often correlate with gaze [37, 79, 175], which suggests that some of the techniques employed in gaze tracking studies could have analogs suitable for use with cursor tracking data. If so, this could allow inexpensive and large-scale usability testing to be carried out "in the wild" using analysis methods that could previously only be used in laboratory-based settings. In Chapter 6, we describe recent work using mouse movement to assess some of the user engagement characteristics listed in Section 1.3 (focus attention, affect, etc.). Next, we focus on studies using mouse movement—solely—in the search domain.

3.4.2   MOUSE MOVEMENT IN SEARCH

Cursor tracking studies have looked at ways in which cursor movements can be used to understand search behavior, the relevance of search results on the search result pages and by themselves.

Mouse Movement and Search Behavior

User behavior on the search result page, when combined with page dwell time and session level information, have been shown to significantly improve result ranking e.g., [5]. Guo et al. [70] showed that cursor movements provide additional clues to predict the success of a search session as a whole. The authors identified patterns of examination and interaction behavior that correlated with users' explicit judgements of search success. Thus, accounting for mouse movement on the search result pages provided information complementary to queries submitted to the search engine, clicks on search results and the amount of time users spend on the pages in a search session. For instance, they demonstrated that the mouse cursor positions in an unsuccessful session were more spread out than in a successful session and spread to the lower part of the result page. The latter suggests that when users examine multiple search results (especially the lower-ranked ones) before a click, they are more likely to be unsuccessful in finding the needed information.

Mouse Movement on Search Result Pages

In a large-scale study, Huang et al. [81] summarized how cursor activity (clicks on a hyperlink, clicks elsewhere, hovering over search result snippet) could be used to estimate the relevance of search results and to differentiate between good and bad abandonment. They showed for instance how hovering over a search result provides indication of relevance in addition to clicks on results. Buscher et al. [33] also examined many types of mouse movements for millions of queries. By clustering users based on cursor features, they identified individual, task, and user-task differences in how users examined results which were similar to those observed in small-scale studies. Within the same context, Lagun et al. [110] proposed the use of frequent *motifs* (cursor movement patterns) extracted using the Dynamic Time Warping distance, which they heavily optimized to scale up. Using motifs, which could be visualized, was shown to be effective to improve document relevance and result ranking. Guo & Agichtein [66] modeled mouse cursor movement and other user interactions to infer whether a search query was navigational or informational.

Finally, Diaz et al. [46] developed mouse movement models capable of estimating user attention on novel search result page layouts (those not deployed yet). These models can help improve search result page design by anticipating users' engagement patterns given a proposed layout. They demonstrated the efficacy of their method using a large set of mouse tracking data collected from two independent commercial search engines.

Search behavior data such as result clickthrough, dwell time, and sequences of searches have widely been used for predicting search success. These approaches however cannot inform how users actually view and interact with the visited result pages (the actual search result a user has clicked on). For example, a search session with a high clickthrough rate would typically be considered a successful search. However, the clickthrough information should be coupled with time information to have a better understanding of the search success. For example, a shorter time before a click may be indicative of higher confidence in the perceived relevance about the search result, while shorter time spent on the landing page might suggest that the user decided that a document was actually not relevant. We focus on the user interaction with the search result next.

Mouse Movement on a Search Result

Using page dwell time for inferring relevance has led to mixed conclusions. Some of the first research was by Morita & Shinoda [138], who conducted a study where participants were asked to provide explicit feedback about the interestingness of news articles that they read. The study focused on the correlation between reading time and explicit feedback while considering document length and additional textual features. The authors found that there was a strong tendency to spend more time on interesting articles rather than on uninteresting ones. Similar findings have also been reported in [42] and [60]. Furthermore, they found only a very weak correlation between the lengths of articles and associated reading times, indicating that most articles were only read in parts, not in their entirety.

Kelly & Belkin [97] tried to reproduce the results of Morita & Shinoda in a complex search scenario, yet found no correlations between display time and explicit relevance ratings for a document. In a subsequent study [98], they again found no general relationship between display time and the users' explicit ratings of the documents' usefulness. Instead, they observed high variation of display time with respect to different users and different tasks. Adjusting for display time according to task type did lead to improved retrieval performance, while adjusting the thresholds according to individual users' degraded performance [208]. In summary, while dwell time clearly contains some relevance signal, previous studies have found many different interpretations of it with no clear consensus about its relationship to document relevance. Indeed, spending a long time on a landing page might suggest that the user was struggling and could not find the relevant information. Sometimes, spending less time on a landing page might suggest that the searcher was actually successful and quickly found the needed information. Hence the suggestion of using mouse movement to indicate relevance.

Claypool et al. [42], who recorded activity from 75 students browsing over 2,500 webpages, found that cursor travel time was a positive indicator of the relevance of a webpage, but they could only differentiate highly irrelevant webpages. They also found that the number of mouse clicks on a page did not correlate with its relevance. This may come as a surprise, but users may be attracted to browse beyond a webpage, and this action can be independent of webpage relevance. Shapira et al. [184] recorded cursor activity from a small number of company employees browsing the web and found that the ratio of mouse movement to reading time was a better indicator of page quality than cursor travel distance and overall length of time that users spend on a page. Finally, Guo & Agictien [69] successfully combined mouse movements with dwell time; these combined metrics were better able to predict document relevance. Mouse movements allowed distinguishing whether a document was "read" as opposed to "scanned" based on dwell time; unsurprisingly reading was a stronger sign of a document relevance than scanning.

Results reported in this section indicate the potential of mouse movement to determine document relevance in the search context. This is important, since the success of a search engine lies in its ability to return relevant results to users. We discuss the use of mouse tracking in contexts other than search next.

3.4.3   MOUSE MOVEMENT ELSEWHERE

Mouse movement has been studied to inform various types of user engagement with web content, in particular to infer user interests in webpages e.g., [63]. We already reported the work of Shapira et al. [184], who found that the ratio of mouse movement to time spent on a webpage was a good indicator of how interested users were in the webpage content.

A small-scale study carried out by Mueller & Lockerd [140] showed that 35% of the users moved their mouse while reading webpages, suggesting that the mouse might indicate users' focus of attention, and could be used to classify user behaviors such as reading, skimming, scrolling, thinking, and interacting with menus. They also saw that there were common patterns in the way users moved the mouse around the webpage, which allowed them to make more accurate predictions of user interest. The authors could also identify user hesitation on regions of the document (link, text) before clicking. They could then predict, using the mouse movement data, what users' second choice would have been by examining the link upon which they hesitated longest before clicking their first choice (users were asked to buy CD/DVD of their choice on two e-shopping sites).

Navalpakkam & Churchill [142] explored the extent to which mouse tracking can inform about whether users are attentive to certain content when reading it, and what their experience is. Their study involved webpages with multimedia content and included text, images, and display advertisements. They also investigated how the mouse behaved when users are distracted, by showing them flickering ads during their reading tasks. They predicted with reasonably high accuracy whether a user was distracted, frustrated, or had an unpleasant experience.

Finally, mouse tracking has been used to study other cognitive processes. For instance, when hand motion was tracked by mouse movement, slow and arched mouse trajectories were shown to indicate an ambiguous state of mind during decision-making [61]. Similar effects have been observed with users confronted with choosing between simple perceptual decision-making tasks [187]. These findings suggest that hand movements, such as those tracked by a mouse, are intertwined with mental processing, and therefore, could potentially reveal how a user's mental state unfolds during their interaction, which is significant for the study of user engagement.

All these studies suggest that mouse movements can reveal important cognitive processes. However, recent work showed that mouse movement gave no or little indication of user attention during relevance assessment tasks [186], indicating that not all cognitive processes can be modeled by mouse movement.

3.5   SUMMARY

This chapter reviews physiological approaches that have been and could be used to measure user engagement. We started by describing measures based on psychophysiology, which focus on the relationship between physiological processes and thoughts, emotions, and behavior. Examples of measurements shown to assess various levels of engagement (relaxation versus stress) include skin conductance level and electromyographic.

The bulk of this chapter focused on two types of physiological measurement, eye tracking and mouse, or more generally cursor tracking. Eye tracking is the process of recording the point of gaze and eye motion. Mouse tracking is the process of collecting users' mouse cursor positions on the computer. A large amount of work involving eye tracking and mouse tracking has been done in the context of search, where engagement centers around the user being satisfied with the search results, or, more precisely, how eye tracking and mouse tracking provide signals about the relevance of the search results. Satisfying user information needs is important, as it indirectly has a positive effect on user loyalty to the search engine. Investigations outside the search scenario exist, showing the potential of mouse tracking in measuring user engagement more broadly. We return to this in Chapter 6, where we report current works mapping mouse tracking recordings to qualitative aspects of user engagement (elicited through questionnaires).

Using physiological measures has many advantages. They are able to produce more objective data, as they do not depend on what the users say or recall about their experience (a problem with think after protocols—see Section 2.4). The measurement can also be performed continuously while the users are performing the task designed to acquire insights about their engagement (e.g., reading news, searching for answers). Finally, physiological measures can provide information about users' emotional and attentional responses that users may not be aware of.

Physiological measures are not without issues. They require equipment, which are often expensive for researchers, and invasive, cumbersome, and obtrusive for participants. The exception to this is mouse tracking, which can be done through a software running on the client side of a computer (a web browser). In addition, there is rarely a one-to-one correspondence between specific behaviors and physiological responses (experiencing joy may affect several body functions of a user, and vice versa, a user's body function may be an indication of more than one type of experience). Related to this, it is usually difficult to operationalize and isolate a physiological construct. Moreover inter-session engagement cannot be accounted for; how to assess why users would want to use a technology again cannot really be measured. Finally, many of the measurements cannot be applied large-scale, apart again for mouse tracking.

With respect to the latter, we should note that it may possible to discover a lot about how users "behave" online from their cursor data, and this creates a significant privacy issue. This issue is complicated by the fact that cursor data can be tracked without the user's knowledge or consent. However, the limitations of cursor tracking technology suggests that this is currently infeasible. For example, the study reported in [203] recorded 20 minutes of data for each of the 350 participants at 24 frames per second (this study is discussed in 6.4), which created over 500MB of data and 300MB of cached webpages. As the large-scale tracking of cursor movements is currently prohibitively expensive, privacy is not expected to be a particularly significant issue with current technology, but may be in the future. For further reading on privacy in the online world, see the Wikipedia entry on "Internet Privacy."[5]

Finally, it is important to ask what type of physiological behaviors in the context of "normal" user engagement can be measured this way. If we look at Plutchik's wheel of emotions [165], engagement in our context is most likely to relate to those emotions at the outer part of the wheel. These include anticipation (as humans, we are curious), joy (when we are happy, we are more likely to want to repeat the experience), and trust (we want to feel safe when interacting with the application). Negative ones include boredom, distraction, and so on. The emotions found at the center of the wheel, which include terror, rage, ecstasy, and amazement, are not likely to be relevant in most "normal experience."

It is likely that physiology measurements are likely to work better for "more extreme" emotions. Examples include: a patient with a psychiatric disorder (such as depersonalization disorder), strong emotion caused by an intense experience (a play where the audience is part of the stage, or riding a roller coaster), or total immersion (while playing a computer game), which actually goes beyond engagement. In addition, to measure user engagement for the "average" users and experiences (e.g., users who visit a news site on a daily basis to consume the latest news), we may actually require conducting "large-ish scale" studies to obtain significant insights. How large-ish is

---

[5]http://en.wikipedia.org/wiki/Internet_privacy.

not clear. This is in itself an interesting and important question to ask, a question to keep in mind when exploring these types of measurement, as they are still expensive to conduct, cumbersome, and obtrusive.

CHAPTER 4

Approaches Based on Web Analytics

Measurements of user engagement using web analytics refer to the extraction of parameters thought to affect user engagement, from the digital traces left by users while interacting with a website, often referred to as website logs.

Self-report measures and physiological measures are usually applied to a relatively small number of users who are thought to be representative of the entire population. In contrast, the approaches based on web analytics are generally applied to the entire population of users on a website. However, the measurements collected by web analytics are necessarily less in-depth, and usually rely on measurements which are proxy for the real factors we wish to know about. For example, the time it takes for a user to read a page (dwell time) is frequently taken as a measure for user interest in the page, even though other factors such as reading level and page length will affect dwell time. Nonetheless, although these measures cannot explicitly explain why users engage with a site, the fact that, for example, two million users choose to access a site daily is a strong indication of a high engagement with that site. Furthermore, by varying specific aspects of the site, e.g., structure and layout, and assessing the effect on user online behavior on the site, these measures can provide implicit understanding on why users engage with the site.

This chapter starts by differentiating two types of web analytics measures, assessing user engagement within a session and across sessions, respectively. We then discuss other dimensions that have been associated with using web analytics to measure user engagement. We then describe a number of measures, and give examples about how to interpret them.

4.1 INTRA-SESSION VS. INTER-SESSION ENGAGEMENT

Intra-session engagement measures can be used to assess our success in attracting users to remain on a website for as long as possible. In comparison, inter-session measures, which take into account multiple sessions, can help in measuring the long-term satisfaction of users with a website. Since in most cases the goal is to have users return to the site again and again, and to perceive the site as beneficial to them, inter-session measures are often more useful than intra-session ones.

Intra-session measures can easily mislead, especially when they are observed for only a short period of time [105]. For example, Kohavi et al. [105] considered the case of a very poor ranking function introduced into a search engine by mistake. This ranking function resulted in irrelevant results being provided to the users. However, because their expectation was that the search engine was providing mostly relevant results, users would assume it was their fault, and would continuously try to submit other queries to the search engine. If a controlled experiment (also known as a bucket test and A/B testing) was run to compare this ranking function to a previously tested one, intra-session measures such as dwell time or number of queries submitted would show a remarkable improvement where, in fact, users were dissatisfied, and might not return to use the search engine.

Inter-session engagement can be measured directly (for example, by tracking the time until a user returns to visit a site) or, for commercial sites, by observing lifetime customer value. Some studies [122] have found correlations between inter- and intra-session measures. For example, in data from a set of Yahoo sites, dwell time (an intra-session measure) and the number of active days (an inter-session measure) had a Spearman correlation of $\rho = -0.66$. This may suggest some redundancy between inter- and intra-session measures. However, as mentioned above, significant differences exist between the two, and in most cases, inter-session measures are to be preferred, or at the very least, should be used in conjunction with intra-session measures.

4.2   SOME DIMENSIONS OF ONLINE MEASUREMENTS

User engagement is not monolithic. It depends on the site analyzed, on the attributes of the users who visit it, and on the task they had in mind when visiting the site. In the following sections we discuss the effects of these parameters on user engagement, and show that it is important to take them into account when measuring user engagement in a web setting, and in particular when interpreting the measurements.

4.2.1   DEPENDENCE ON THE TYPE OF WEBSITE

The type of website one is measuring has a cardinal effect on engagement measures. For example, a news site will see different engagement patterns compared to those of an online shopping site. While the former will likely see repeated visits during the day, and possibly short star-like visitation patterns within sessions (if the site contains links to other websites), the latter is more likely to show longer, more widely spaced sessions.

It is unsurprising, then, that studies have shown such variations, even in sites with similar designs, from similar providers. Yom-Tov et al. [211] showed that the average dwell time (defined in Section 4.4.1) for 50 major Yahoo sites varies significantly. The sites with the shortest dwell time include sports sites (e.g., checking the latest sport results), whereas the highest average dwell time was recorded on leisure sites (e.g., reading about travel destinations).

Similarly, Lehmann et al. [122] showed that websites could be clustered by engagement measures. They show that sites differ widely in terms of their engagement. Some sites were very popular (e.g., news sites) whereas others are visited by small groups of users (e.g., specific interest sites). Time spent on the site also depended on the sites, e.g., search sites tended to have a much shorter dwell time than sites related to entertainment (e.g., games). Loyalty per site differed as well. Media (news, magazines) and communication (e.g., messenger, mail) had many users returning to them much more regularly than sites containing information of temporary interests (e.g., buying a car). Loyalty was also influenced by the frequency in which new content is published (e.g., some sites produce new content once per week).

4.2.2   DEPENDENCE ON THE TYPE OF USER

Studies have shown that users may arrive at a site by accident or through exploration, and simply never return. Other users may visit a site once a month, for example a credit card site to check their balance. On the other hand, sites such as mail may be accessed by many users on a daily basis. Finally, each website has different appeals to different audiences. Therefore, we can expect different users to exhibit different modes of engagements. This has been observed, for example, in a study by Lehmann et al. [122], where users were partitioned according to the number of days per month that a site is used:

1. Tourists: 1 day

2. Interested: 2–4 days

3. Average: 5–8 days

4. Active: 9–15 days

5. VIP: more than 16 days

A sample of 80 websites ranging from media to mail to shopping were then clustered according to the proportion of users from each group who visit the site. Figure 4.1 shows the resulting clustering. It is clear that different sites receive different user types and, hence, corresponding usage. We observe that the proportion of tourist users is high for all sites. The top cluster has the highest proportion of tourist users; typical sites include special events (e.g., the Oscars) or those related to configuration. The second from the top cluster includes sites related to specific information that are occasionally needed; as such they are not visited regularly within a month. The third cluster includes sites related to e-commerce, media, which are used on a regular basis, albeit not daily. Finally, the bottom cluster contains navigation sites (e.g., homepage) and communication sites (e.g., messenger). For these sites, the proportion of VIP users is higher than the proportion of active and average users.

The above indicates that the type of users, e.g., tourist versus VIP, matters when measuring engagement. For instance, it may be preferable to focus on measuring engagement for those users that are of interest, e.g., to the website company (for example, focusing solely on VIP users or ignoring tourist users), and that in general it is false to assume that engagement is identical for all users of a website.

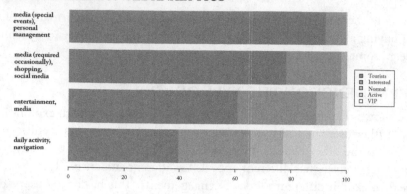

Figure 4.1: Proportion of users from different groups in a sample of 80 sites (from [122]).

4.2.3 DEPENDENCE ON THE TASK

Engagement varies by task. A user who accesses a website to check for emails (a goal-specific task) has different engagement patterns from one who is browsing for leisure. This is one reason why engagement patterns vary during different times of the day, as peoples' task and as a consequence engagement with specific sites vary during recreational and business hours [22, 122].

In one study [211], sessions in which 50% or more of the visited sites belonged to the five most common sites (for each user) were classified as goal-specific. Goal-specific sessions accounted for 38% of sessions, and were predominantly related to email, search, and social networks. Most users (92%) had both goal-specific and non-goal-specific sessions. Interestingly, the average downstream engagement (see Section 5.2) in goal-specific sessions was 25% lower compared to non-goal-specific sessions. Moreover, the design of websites had a smaller effect on engagement during goal-specific sessions. Thus, when users do not have specific goals in mind, they may be more ready to accept suggestions for additional browsing which increases engagement. Thus, a better measure of engagement can be obtained by estimating the context of the user and their intended task.

4.3 LARGE-SCALE MEASUREMENTS

Many measures have been proposed for large-scale measurement of user engagement. They are distinct in that they rely on parameters that can be easily collected from website logs or through simple instrumentation of webpages. Table 4.1 shows a list of commonly used measures for estimating user engagement, partitioned by whether they apply to single sites or to multiple sites (usually, of the same provider), and whether they measure intra-session engagement, or inter-session engagement.

One obvious observation from Table 4.1 is that engagement measures are predominantly single-site measures. There is a dearth of multi-site measures, which have only started to be re-

Table 4.1: Different measures for large-scale online user engagement

	Single site	Multiple sites
Intra-session measures	Dwell time (session duration) Clickthrough rate (CTR) Number of pages viewed (click depth) Conversion rate (mostly for e-commerce) Number of comments (on social media sites) Play time (on video sites) Mouse movements (sometimes)	Revisits Cumulative activity Activity pattern Downstream engagement Complex network metrics
Inter-session measures	Fraction of return visits Time between visits (inter-session time, absence time) Lifetime value (number of actions) Number of sessions per unit of time Total usage time per unit of time Number of friends on site (in social networks) Number of views (on video sites) Total view time per month (on video sites)	

searched in the last few years. We return to this in Chapter 5. In this chapter, we restrict ourselves to single-site measures. Second, while many measures are applicable to any site, some measures are tailored to specific site types, such as video sites, e-commerce, etc.

Lehmann et al. [122] suggested a different partition of engagement measures, according to the following attributes (we already mentioned some of them in Section 4.2):

1. Popularity: Popularity metrics measure how much a site is used. For example, the total number of users to a site, number of visits, and number of clicks to a site. The higher the number, the more popular the corresponding site.

2. Activity: How a site is used is measured with activity metrics. For example, the number of page views per visit, and the time per visit (dwell time).

3. Loyalty: Loyalty metrics are concerned with how often users return to a site. For example, the number of days a user visits a site, number of times visited, and the total time spent on the site.

Loyalty and popularity metrics depend on the considered time interval, e.g., number of weeks considered. A highly engaging site is one with a high number of visits (popular), where users spend lots of time (active), and return frequently (loyal). The advantage of this categorization is that each of these categories captures a different facet of engagement, and they are therefore not highly correlated.

In the following two sections, we describe in detail single-site measures, intra-session and inter-session, respectively.

4.4   INTRA-SESSION MEASUREMENTS

In this section, we present some of the most used single-site intra-session measures.

4.4.1   DWELL TIME AND SIMILAR MEASURES

Dwell time is the contiguous length of time that users spend on a webpage or a website. When applied to a website, this measure is also known as session duration, as the user may leave but return to the website within the same session. A session is a sequence of pages visited by a user until he or she goes offline. Following [34], the most commonly adopted definition of a session is that it ends if more than 30 minutes have elapsed between two successive activities of that user. As a measure of single-site, intra-session engagement, dwell time or session duration is probably the most widely used measure for online engagement. It is also used in the context of search (both organic and sponsored) as a proxy of post-click user satisfaction e.g., [21, 103].

Dwell time has recently been reported to complement and even replace click-based signals when recommending content items to users. The amount of time that users spend on content items was shown to be a good indication of user interest in the items [210]. The authors had to address many challenges such as the effect of the item length, the type of item (slideshow versus articles), and users' content consumption behaviors.

Dwell time has a long-tailed distribution, similar to a lognormal distribution. Figure 4.2 shows the distribution of dwell times per page for a sample of users on 50 websites [211]. This data was extracted from a large sample of anonymized interaction data (tuples of browser cookie, URL, and timestamp) from users who gave their consent to provide browsing data through the toolbar of a large Internet company. These users represent a sample of users across the world who access that company and many other websites. As this figure shows, while the mode of the distribution is around 30 seconds, there are significant numbers of very short sessions (under 10 seconds) and very long ones (over 100 seconds in length).

Figure 4.3 shows the average dwell time for the same 50 websites. Dwell time varies significantly between websites. Leisure sites tend to have longer dwell times than news, e-commerce, etc. As this figure shows, average dwell times can range from around 15 seconds to over 2 minutes. Additionally, dwell time has a relatively large variance even for the same site, very likely depending on user types (see Section 4.2.2). Thus, care should be taken when comparing dwell times across websites and user groups.

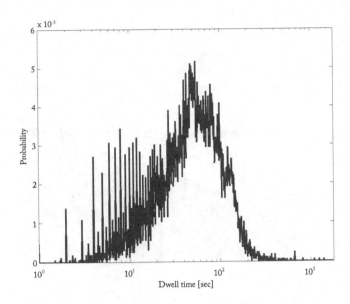

Figure 4.2: Distribution of dwell time per page on a sample of 50 websites.

There are variants of dwell time for specific kinds of websites and media. Play time [47] is used for measuring dwell-time-like engagement in video sites (e.g., YouTube.com). The number of comments on social media sites [22] is a proxy for the length of time spent on these sites.

A different measure based on dwell time is bounce rate, which can be defined in two ways. When a user arrives at a website, he or she may decide to not go any further; there are no clicks on the website. Another definition is when a user stays less than a defined threshold time on the site, for example leaving within 2 seconds of landing on the website. Bounce rate is the percentage of such instances. It is particularly useful for e-commerce sites, as users bouncing is a sign that they are not interested in what the site has to offer or in the way it is offering it. It is an appropriate measure in the context of advertisements (i.e., as a proxy of post-click satisfaction) [183].

Although dwell time is a popular measure, there are significant drawbacks in using it. First, as noted above, it is a single session measure. More importantly, it is not clear that the user was actually looking at the site while he or she was there. Users may have been distracted, or may have been using a different tab of the browser to look at other websites [80, 121]. Therefore, measurements of dwell time can be noisy. Finally, websites which aggregate content of other sites (e.g., news aggregators) direct the user to visiting those sites and return for more links. In such cases, the actual dwell time is divided between multiple page visits, and it may be more appropriate to use measures such as the number of revisits within session (see next).

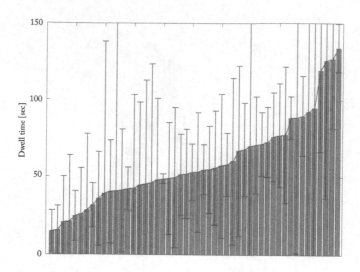

Figure 4.3: The average dwell time per website for a sample of 50 websites.

4.4.2 REVISITS TO A SITE

User revisits within a session occur when a user leaves the website of interest and returns to it at a later time during the session. Such revisits are common in sites which are browser homepages, that contain content which is of regular interest to users, or aggregate links to other sites, e.g., news aggregators like news.microsoft.com. Conversely, goal-oriented sites (e.g., e-commerce) have lower within-session revisit rates. Thus, for aggregator type-sites, revisits may be more reflective of engagement than dwell time.

Users often revisiting one site during an online session may be due to the fact that are effectively engaging in multitasking. Lehmann et al. [121] study the browsing data of 2.5M users across 760 sites encompassing diverse types of services such as social media, news, and mail, and show that revisitation patterns vary depending on the type of websites. Sites with the highest number of revisits within a session belong to the social media category, whereas news tech sites are the least revisited sites. From these and other insights related to revisitation patterns, they propose metrics that characterize multitasking during online sessions and show how they provide additional insights to standard engagement metrics such as dwell time. We return to this in Section 5.1.

4.4.3 CLICKTHROUGH RATE

Online advertisers commonly utilize pay-per-performance systems, where payment to a website (or ads agency) is based on the number of clicks that an advertisement received, compared to the number of times it was shown [173]. This measure of performance is known as the clickthrough rate (CTR), and is computed as the number of clicks on an advertisement divided by the number of times it was shown.

A direct measure of engagement with an advertisement should be computed as a function of the conversion rate (see below), which CTR does not directly measure. Instead, CTR uses the fact that a user clicked on the advertisement (rather than making a purchase) as the proxy for conversion. Nevertheless, CTR is widely used in the advertising industry, because of the ease of measuring it.

Though CTR is usually associated with measuring engagement in advertising, it has been used elsewhere. Ponnuswami et al. [166] attempted to optimize different modules of a search engines, e.g., organic search results, news, or images. These modules (also known as verticals) can either be displayed or not and results from them may be clicked by the user, if they contain relevant results. Thus, CTR is a useful measure for engagement in this scenario. Additionally, since verticals are usually browsed in sequence, the fact that a user clicked on a vertical below another vertical which was not clicked is of importance in itself, because it implies that the user saw a vertical, but chose not to engage with its results. Ponnuswami et al. [166] termed this a "normalized vertical CTR."

Finally, CTR has been used extensively in the context of search engines, but more as an indication of the quality of the search results returned to the users, thus their relevance, and less about the engagement of the users with search engine. However, returning relevant results to users, thus satisfying their information needs, is what will make the users engage long term with the search tool.

4.4.4 NUMBER OF PAGES VIEWED

Number of pages viewed or click depth is measured by counting the number of pages visited within a site during a session, or the percentage of sessions where more than a given number of pages were visited within a site [86]. This measure is particular useful for sites providing content to consume (such as news websites) where the aim is for user to access and hopefully read lots of content on offer by the site, which can be accessed by clicking on the links posted on the site (headline, related stories, editor's pick, etc., for a news website).

In some ways, click depth is complementary to measuring revisits, because it disregards the number of off-site visits during a session. However, one should be cautious using this measure because a poorly designed website will require users to navigate into many more pages than necessary, decreasing user engagement while seemingly having users strongly engaged with the site [105].

4.4.5   OTHER MEASUREMENTS

Depending on the specific audience of a website and its goal, as well as available information, other engagement measures than the ones described above may be preferred or used in addition. The most important example is in e-commerce sites. The goal of these sites (by definition) is to sell products to a user. Thus, it is not enough that a user browses many pages in the site, returns to it often, or spends a considerable amount of time browsing it. The most direct measure of the success of an e-commerce site is the purchasing of a product using the site. Therefore, e-commerce sites frequently measure conversion rate, which is the fraction of sessions which end in a desired user action (e.g., purchasing a product, downloading a software package, registering to an emailing list).

Not all sessions are expected to result in a conversion. In some cases, site owners may be interested in increasing awareness to the site or in convincing a user to recommend the sites to friends, so conversion rate is not always the singular measure of engagement. However, conversion rate has the advantage of being closer to a website manager's goal. However, for conversion to happen, users need to spend time on the site. As a result, dwell time and bounce rate are often used in addition to conversion rate in e-commerce sites.

As presented in Section 3.4, laboratory studies have shown that people use the mouse cursor for a variety of uses beyond clicking on links. For example, cursor movement is used to mark interesting results [81, 175]. More importantly, mouse cursor movement has been shown (in small-scale studies) to correlate well with eye movement [37]. Hence, when a website can be instrumented to capture mouse movement, this can provide an interesting measure of single-session engagement. Note that mouse movement does not always need to be captured at a very high definition. Sometimes, even a rough measure such as whether the user hovered above a module in the page can suffice to obtain useful information.

As already discussed in Section 3.4, several such studies exist, mostly for optimizing search engine results. One reason for this is that search engines frequently show all required information on the search result itself. This means users do not have to click on a link to obtain the information they are seeking, thus removing an important signal of relevance to search engine operators. In studies such as reported in [81], mouse tracking was shown to properly indicate engagement and relevance without requiring users to click on the links displayed on a page.

4.5   INTER-SESSION MEASUREMENTS

Inter-session measures take into account user engagement across multiple sessions. Since in most cases the goal of a website operator is to have users engaging with the site for more than a single session, measuring long-term engagement (and hence satisfaction) of a user with a site is of primary importance. Therefore, even though such measures usually require a longer data collection phase, they are very important as they provide crucial information not available with intra-session measures. Inter-session measures can be categorized into three groups:

1. Direct value measurements

2. Total use measurements

3. Return-rate measurements

In the following we explain each of these categories, and provide examples for them.

4.5.1   DIRECT VALUE MEASUREMENT

Direct value measurements evaluate the perceived value of a customer as calculated by the website operator. Some sites have a relatively simple goal for engaging with a user. For example, e-commerce sites might consider the value of a customer to be comprised of the total sum of sales made to the customer.

This definition of engagement is easy to explain, but it is not always easy for a website operator to decide on. For example, a cellphone manufacturer website might consider the value of a customer to be derived from the revenue generated by sales to the customer, but the website also has an important role in addressing customer support. Therefore, revenue might not reflect all the facets of engagement necessary to measure user engagement. Another problem with direct value measurements is that it can be difficult to measure the effect of minor changes to the website on customer engagement, except for very special circumstances.

Common measures of direct value usually comprise of the total customer lifetime value, as measured by revenue, ads clicked, monetization, etc.

4.5.2   TOTAL USE MEASUREMENT

When the value of a customer is difficult to define, website operators may resort to measuring user engagement by observing the use of the website by the customer over long periods of time and across multiple sessions. Examples of total use measures include the total usage time by the user per unit of time and the number of sessions per unit of time. Specific websites such as video sites use a slight modification of this measure, namely the total view time per month [47].

Social network sites monitor the total number of friends on the site [51]. One reason for this is that it is known that the density of friendship ties in a social network grows over time [85]. Hence, if users are engaged with the social network site, we should expect to see the number of friends grow over time.

Similar to the direct value measurement, it can be hard to measure the effect of minor changes to a website with total use measurement. However, they are easier to use than direct value measures, because they rely on events that are likely to happen more frequently (e.g., user visiting the site) than actual conversions (e.g., user making a purchase).

4.5.3   RETURN-RATE MEASUREMENT

Websites whose goal is to engage users by having them visit the sites on a regular basis, for example, news sites, social media sites, and email providers, can directly measure the success of this goal. Two types of return-rate measurements have been proposed in the literature. First, one could measure the fraction of return visits to the site, that is, how many users return for another visit following their latest visit? Second, we can measure the time between consecutive visits of a user. These measures are also known as user loyalty, inter-session time, or absence time [48].

Dupret & Lalmas [48] used absence time to measure the effectiveness of different ranking functions in the search engine of Yahoo Answers. User behavior was modeled using a hazard model, which is a natural way to model return rates, because the model can accommodate both users who return to the site (together with the time it took them to return) and users who do not return to the site, by labeling these users as unobserved. This study found several interesting relationships between absence time and intra-session behaviors. For example, the number of clicks (click depth) during a session increased engagement for the first few clicks, but decayed after the fifth click, which is possibly similar to the findings of Kohavi et al. [105].

Thus, return rate measures are an important measure of engagement, especially when users are expected to return to a site within a relatively short time.

4.6   SUMMARY

This chapter reviewed measurement approaches based on web analytics. The focus was on single-site measurement, with respect to intra-session and inter-session visits to a website. Examples of measures include number of unique users, click-through rates, page views, user revisits, dwell time, absence time. These measures aim at capturing three important facets of a site engagement: popularity, loyalty, and activity. Although these measures actually measure web usage, they are commonly employed as a proxy for online user engagement: the higher and the more frequent the usage, the more engaged the user. Major websites and online services are compared using these and other similar engagement metrics, as they have been used for many years by Internet marketing research companies (e.g., comScore).[1]

This and the previous two chapters described the three main approaches currently in use or put forward to measure engagement in the online context: self-reporting, physiological, and finally on web analytics. For each, we provided examples of studies that have utilized them in the measurement of engagement or related constructs, and highlighted their strengths and limitations.

These approaches represent various trade-offs between scale of data and depth of understanding. For instance, surveys—self-reported method—are small-scale but deep, whereas clicks—web analytics—are large-scale but shallow in understanding. Little work has been done to integrate these various measures into a coherent understanding of engagement success. There

---

[1]http://www.comscore.com.

are however various efforts looking at these various approaches, aiming to gain insights from big data with deep analysis of human behavior. These are described in Chapter 6. Before going forward, however, we wish to introduce some caveats in our discussion of measurement, namely, how do we move beyond focusing on users interacting with a single online application on a single, stationary device?

In addition, the ubiquitous computing environment offers challenges for the measurement of user engagement, and its future agenda cannot be discussed without considering, "what's beyond the desktop?"

CHAPTER 5

Beyond Desktop, Single Site, and Single Task

This chapter looks at measuring user engagement in more complex scenarios, acknowledging the ubiquitous computing environment.

In the previous three chapters, we looked at user engagement at the site level and implicitly at the task level: a user visits a website or uses an application to perform a task, spends time on the site/with the application, and returns to it later on when needed to perform the same or a similar task. Examples of sites include a news site and an email site and examples of tasks include reading a news article and processing an email, respectively. We described three types of approaches to measure user engagement, through self-reporting where users are asked about their engagement experience (Chapter 2), physiological measurement where physical reactions to cognitive or affective states are recorded and analyzed (Chapter 3), and web analytics, where the depth of engagement of millions of users on a website is expressed through inter- and intra-session metrics (Chapter 4).

However engagement goes beyond this single-site and single-task scenario. Users, when online, may not just visit one site, but several sites. They may want to access several websites to accomplish a task (e.g., comparing flights across various travel websites) or they are simply browsing several sites for unrelated reasons (e.g., reading emails then reading news then back to the email site). The first two sections of this chapter focus on these multi-site and multi-task scenarios. First we define the concept of online multitasking, show its effect, and describe how web analytics metrics have been adapted to account for it. We then study this concept in the context of sites offered by large Internet service providers, where the aim is to keep users engaged with their sites, and how to measure this type of engagement.

The previous three chapters have also focused on measuring user engagement when users interact with websites from their desktop. However, users spend an increasing amount of their time online, not sitting in front of their desktop, but through their mobile phones or tablets. The third section of this chapter looks at user engagement in that context.

5.1 MEASURING FOR ONLINE MULTITASKING

When users are performing a task on the web (e.g., planning a holiday), they may visit several sites (e.g., to compare offers from different travel sites, read reviews of accommodations) within an online session. A user may access several sites to perform a main task or may actually perform

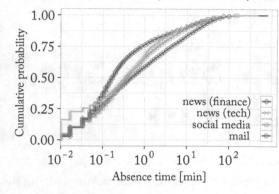

	#Visits		Absence time [min]	
news (finance)	2.09	4.65	3.85	14.00
news (tech)	1.76	1.59	3.95	14.16
social media	2.28	4.78	4.47	14.11
mail	2.09	4.61	6.86	18.53

Figure 5.1: Site visit characteristics for four categories of sites: (Left) Distribution of time between visits; and (Right) Average and standard deviation of number of visits and time between visits (*avg*|*sd*) (from [121]).

several totally unrelated tasks in parallel (e.g., responding to an email while reading news). This is referred to as *online multitasking* [121].

Online multitasking has been studied in the context of web search [127, 189]. For instance, Spink et al. [189] observed that multitasking occurred in 81% of sessions. Wang et al. [202] showed that 92% of the participants in their study had online sessions where they accessed several sites to perform between 2 to 8 tasks. Other studies provided various insights about this phenomenon. For instance, from a large-scale analysis of user online browsing sessions, it was found that users accessed different sites during a session [108] and a large proportion of pages were visited more than once. Revisitation rate was found to be around 81% in 2001 [135] and 73% in 2005 [77]. In addition, the frequency at which a page was revisited differed depending on the user's habits and the type of website (e.g., social media, commerce, etc.) [108, 147], or in other words, the web tasks a user wished to accomplish on the site. Reasons for revisiting included active monitoring of content, verification of information, regular use of online services, and reoccurring tasks. With respect to the latter, three types of revisitation patterns were identified, short-term (backtrack, undo), medium-term (re-utilize, observe), and long-term revisits (rediscover), where it was shown that 73% of revisits were short term. This is in accordance with another study [77] that reported that 74% of revisits were performed within a session. Collectively, these works provide strong evidence that multitasking during online sessions exists and is clearly connected to web tasks.

Lehmann et al. [121] investigated online multitasking with 760 websites, encompassing diverse types of services such as social media, news, and mail. Figure 5.1 shows various statistics for four categories of sites: news (finance), news (tech), social media, and mail: number of visits during a session (how often a website was visited) and time between visits (how long between two visits on the same site). The latter is referred to "absence time" (Section 4.5.3). Sites with the highest number of visits within a session belonged to the social media category, whereas news (tech) sites are the least revisited sites. The news (finance) sites have a skewed distribution, indicating a higher proportion of short absence time for sites in this category. Finally, email sites had the highest absence time. Lehmann et al. also looked at the distributions of the absence time across all categories of sites, and saw that the median was less than 1 minute, and this for all categories. That is, many sites were revisited after a short break.

They speculated that a short break may correspond to an interruption of the task being performed by the user (on the site), whereas a longer break indicated that the user is returning to the site to perform a new task. They therefore proposed a metric to capture this, the *cumulative activity* metric,[1] which accounts for the time between site visits (absence time):

$$CumAct_k = \log_{10}(v_1 + \sum_{i=2}^{n} v_i \cdot iv_i^k)$$

Here v_i corresponds to time spent during the ith visit, iv_i is the absence time between the $(i-1)^{th}$ and i^{th} visit, and n is the number of visits on the site. The value of $CumAct_k$ increases with the time spent between visits to the site. The exponent k is used to scale the iv_i parameter; a high value increases the importance of between-visit activity iv_i. When $k = 0$, the focus is solely on the visits to the site, and $CumAct_0$ corresponds to the total time spent on the site during the whole session, a well-established web analytics metric.

Revisiting a site may mean that the user is returning to continue with the same task; in this case, the "visit" to the site is actually splits into several sub-visits, and should be viewed as one visit. The longer the time between two visits, the higher the likelihood that the user is returning to the site to perform a similar type of task, albeit a new one (e.g., a new search for a different information need). This somewhat reflects the loyalty of the user to the site, and the cumulative activity metric increases the importance of visits that preceded a longer break of activity on that site.

Lehmann et al. [121] also saw that the time spent on mail sites decreased at each revisit; the opposite pattern was observed for social media sites. A possible explanation for this is that, for mail sites, there were fewer messages to read in subsequent visits, whereas for social media sites, users spent longer at each subsequent visit because they are done with what they wanted to do (reading their emails, reading news) and have time to see what their "friends" are posting and interact with them.

News (finance) is an example of category for which neither a lower nor higher dwell time was observed at each subsequent revisit. The hypothesis was that each visit corresponded to either a new task or a user following some evolving piece of information such as checking the latest stock price figures. For news (tech) sites, Lehmann et al. either found no patterns, or the pattern was complex and could not easily be described. However, they saw that for both the first two visits or the last two visits, in both cases, a higher dwell time was observed for each second visit. This

---

[1]Other activity metrics could be used (see Section 4.3). Here for illustration, we use dwell time on a site.

may indicate that the visits belonged to two different tasks, and each task was performed in two distinct visits to the site.

They concluded that how long a user spent on a site at the subsequent visits to the site can provide additional information about how users engage with the site. An increase in dwell time can be interpreted as a user getting increasingly more engaged with the site at each revisit, whereas a decrease in dwell time corresponds to a user shifting his or her attention away from the site, arguably because the focus moves to some other task on another site. Finally, a constant dwell time is interpreted as the user repeatedly visiting the site to perform the same type of task. They therefore defined a second metric, referred to as *activity pattern* metric to capture four patterns of *user attention to the site*: decreasing, increasing, constant, and complex (the formulas are omitted). For instance, an increasing attention can reflect "stickiness" at the session level: users are increasingly engaged with the site during the session. The news (tech) case above discussed would be an example of a complex pattern. This new metrics allowed identifying which site followed which pattern.

The authors, in this paper, showed that these two metrics reflect how users engage with a site during the entire session, in the presence of multitasking. They identified different types of behavior and observed that the behavior can differ significantly even between sites of the same category. Some sites are visited to perform a single task during a session. The time between visits is then short and the visits are connected with each other while the user attention shows a particular trend, either shifting toward or away from the site. Other sites are characterized by a steady return of users even after long absence times. In this case the visits tend not to be connected, and the activity pattern is complex: only parts of the visits belong to the same task.

There are however some limitations to the study, as acknowledged by the authors themselves. First, the definition of a task is simplistic and should be extended. For example, to book a holiday, a user may visit several sites within the same session and one site many times across several sessions. Moreover, the way absence time was interpreted needs to be validated: user is returning to a site to continue with the same task (continue reading the news articles)—associated with short absence time—or to start a totally different task (a new unrelated information need)—associated with long absence time. Works in this direction in the search domain already exist [6, 127].

5.2   MEASURING ON A NETWORK OF SITES

Many online service providers operate multiple content sites. For example, Yahoo operates sites dealing with finance, sports, celebrities, and shopping. Due to the varied content served by these sites, it is difficult to treat them as a single entity. For this reason, they are usually studied and optimized separately. However, it is clear that online service providers should address engagement on the different sites they manages as whole, as sites can point to each other. For example, if a site does not have any links on its pages to other sites of the same provider, users will find it difficult to navigate to them. Conversely, linking to relevant content of the same provider will improve engagement.

On the other hand, and as described in the previous section, users may spend many of their online sessions multitasking, e.g., emailing, reading news, accessing a social network, and generally navigating between sites. Online multitasking has implications when looking at the network of sites offered by online providers, as several of the provider sites can be accessed during a single session. Here, it is about the fact that several such sites are accessed because of online multitasking, than a site being accessed several times, during the same online session. Therefore, site engagement should be examined not only within individual sites, but also across sites, that is, the entire provider network. The engagement that happens because of the interaction between the site and its surrounding network is what is known as *networked user engagement* [211].

Yom-Tov et al. [211] defined a metric to measure this type of engagement, i.e., at the network level. The metric, called *Downstream engagement score* (DES), is the total time spent on provider sites from the next site until the end of the provider session, divided by the total remaining session time. By definition, if the next site in the session is not a provider site, DES is zero. Formally, let S be the set of sites visited during a session. We index the sites S by $i \in 1, 2, \ldots, n$. To compute the DES of site S_i, we introduce a binary indicator $\mathbb{1}_j$ that is 1 if site S_j belongs to the provider of interest *and* if the user did not visit any site not belonging to the provider of interest between his or her visit from sites S_i and S_j. It is 0 otherwise. Let denote by $t(S_i)$ the dwell time spent on site S_i. DES $E(S_i)$ for sessions that contain one provider session[2] is:

$$E(S_i) = \frac{\sum_{j>i} t(S_j)\mathbb{1}_j}{\sum_{j>i} t(S_j)}$$

For example, consider a session where a user visits seven sites out of which only the second, the third, the fourth, and the seventh sites belong to the provider of interest i.e., for the provider session starting at site number 2, the indicator vector is given by:

$$(\mathbb{1}_1, \mathbb{1}_2, \mathbb{1}_3, \mathbb{1}_4, \mathbb{1}_5, \mathbb{1}_6, \mathbb{1}_7) = (0, 1, 1, 1, 0, 0, 0).$$

Then, the DES for S_2 is

$$E(S_2) = \frac{t(S_3) + t(S_4)}{t(S_3) + t(S_4) + t(S_5) + t(S_6) + t(S_7)}$$

The provider session for S_2 contains S_3 and S_4. DES of sites S_1 and S_i with $i \geq 4$ are, by definition, zero. Intuitively, DES measures the fraction of time the users spent on a content provider's sites (network)—without leaving—out of the entire time they had available to spend browsing the Internet (the total session). DES, defined thus, complements previous measurements of single-site engagement.[3]

---

[2]A session in which a site from the provider has been visited.

[3]Several other definitions were also attempted by [211] such as the fraction of time users spent on the provider network out of the total session time. They were found to highly correlate with the one presented in this section, and hence adopted by the authors in their study.

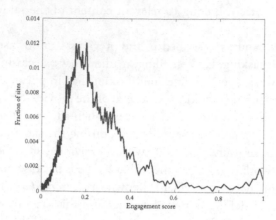

Figure 5.2: Distribution of downstream engagement scores (DES).

Yom-Tov et al. [211] looked at the distribution of DES for a sample of 50 Yahoo sites, which is shown in Figure 5.2 (average: 0.18, standard deviation: 0.14). As the figure shows, this distribution is heavy tailed, with a significant portion of long sessions within the provider network, which indicates a good downstream engagement pattern.

The average DES for 50 sites of the Yahoo network is shown in Figure 5.3. As the figure shows, there is significant variance in engagement, and some sites have a much stronger average downstream engagement than others. The sites with the highest average DES are leisure and sport sites (sites to which users come to spend time on, e.g., to play or read), whereas those with the lowest average engagement are e-commerce and informational sites (sites to which users come for specific purposes, e.g., to purchase or check something).

Some sessions may be more sensitive to changes aimed at increasing downstream engagement level than others. For example, a user who accesses a site to check for emails may be less influenced by additional browsing opportunities from posted links than a user who is browsing for leisure. We call the first kind of sessions goal-specific, and distinguish between goal-specific sessions and all other sessions in the following manner. Yom-Tov et al. used the following procedure to distinguish between the two types of sessions.

For each user, the five most common sites he or she visited during the data collection period were identified. For information, the most frequent common sites were related to mail, search, and social networks. The authors' hypothesis that sessions in which 50% or more of the visited sites belonged to the five most common sites (for that user) could be classified as goal-specific. Goal-specific sessions accounted for 38% of the sessions. Approximately 92% of users had sessions with both kinds of sites. The average downstream engagement in goal-specific sessions was 0.16. This is to be contrasted with a higher average downstream engagement of 0.2 during other sessions.

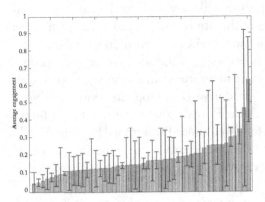

Figure 5.3: Distribution of average downstream engagement scores. Each bar represents a single site. The error bars show one standard deviation across time.

Table 5.1: Spearman correlations between number of links to the same site, links to another provider site, and link to a site outside the provider network, and three measures of engagement

	e-commerce	news
Downstream engagement		
Same site	0.03	-0.31
Other provider sites	-0.09	0.20
Non-provider sites	-0.10	0.04
Dwell time		
Same site	0.51	0.78
Other provider sites	-0.61	0.38
Non-provider sites	-0.51	0.52
Fraction of links		
Same site	0.52	0.19
Other provider sites	0.38	0.72
Non-provider sites	0.10	0.08

This implies that when users do not have specific goals in mind, they may be more ready to accept suggestions (e.g., more links) for additional browsing, and engagement can be influenced this way.

Yom-Tov et al. [212] looked at the effect of *links*, on networked user engagement, as these are commonly used to influence user engagement by, e.g., web-masters and editors. Table 5.1 shows the correlations between three types of links (their numbers) and two engagement metrics, for two sites. The two sites correspond to news and e-commerce. The two metrics are DES and dwell time, which is the total time a user spends visiting contiguous pages within a site (Section 4.4.1). The three types of links are: link to the same site, link to another site within the provider network (Yahoo in this study) and link to a site outside the provider network. The percentages for each type for the two sites are shown in the table.

With respect to the news site, if the aim is to keep users on the site, then having links to the site itself helps (i.e., more news stories to consume). It also seems that when users are on the news site, they are there to read news (if appropriately enticed). Nonetheless, they can be directed to other sites on the network. Providing users with external links does not affect downstream engagement, but it does for dwell time. The authors' hypothesis, which requires verification, was that too many choices cause users to remain where they are. Other reasons are plausible: it might be that adding links to external sites lead the user to believe that the news is well documented and trustworthy.

With respect to the e-commerce site, links have little effect on downstream engagement, whereas they have on dwell time. Dwell time can be increased by having more links into the site itself, and no links to other and external sites. Overall, it seems that, as expected, users of the e-commerce site have a defined intent. Attempts to direct them to additional sites is pointless, for example, by showing extra links. In fact, it hurts the time spent on the site.

Studying inter-site engagement is important for companies offering a diverse range services, such as Yahoo! or AOL, but also for those with fewer services (e.g., LinkedIn, Facebook), or with one main service with several instances of it (e.g., Amazon, Wikipedia). For example, Amazon does not just sell books, but also clothes, furniture, etc.; each of these categories can be viewed as a specific site, and the same methodology can be used to predict downstream engagement across these categories. The Wikipedia project can also benefit from this work. Indeed, Wikipedia offers different functionalities, and each of them can be viewed as a site on its own.

5.3   MEASURING IN MOBILE INFORMATION SEEKING

Within the past decade there has been increasing emphasis on the mobile user experience. Pew Internet Research reports that 91% of American adults own cell phones, and that 56% use their mobiles to access the Internet. In addition to communication activities such as email (50%) and texting (80%), mobile users are also capturing information (taking pictures [82%] and recording videos [44%]) and performing information tasks, such as online banking (29%) and seeking health information (31%) [27]. More and more information and communication functions are performed on mobile devices, and it is therefore not an understatement to say that mobile devices are changing the ways in which we are learning, working, communicating, and socializing in our everyday lives. Understanding mobile user engagement will be critical for supporting these tasks.

Several works, albeit in the context of search, provide interesting insights comparing user behaviors on mobile to those on desktop. For instance, [92, 188] showed that desktop users are usually active during working hours, whereas mobile users are more active during the evening. Search topics are different as well, with mobile users being more likely to search for adult content, celebrities, and images [188]. Search sessions on mobile are shorter than on desktop, confirming results from [3] showing that browsing sessions on mobile were shorter in general. Therefore, mobile browsing behavior differs from that of traditional desktops, and this should be taken into account when measuring user engagement.

Few studies have looked specifically at user engagement with respect to mobile use, though there is a great deal of important work in the user experience literature upon which to model mobile user engagement and consider measurement issues. Two ways to explore mobile user experiences has been to employ diary or log studies, often combining interviews with these methods.

Diary studies have focused on general information access, e.g., [146] and information search behavior more specifically, e.g., [106]. The duration of these studies has typically been between one and four weeks, and they sometimes include an interview component to address both general and study-specific Internet or mobile activities. Diary entries, typically submitted through an online survey, have focused on a range of details, including: users' physical location; purpose or motivation for using the mobile; how they approached the activity, i.e., app used; activity completed using the phone; degree of success in task completion; satisfaction with task completion; time to complete the task; and descriptions of users' social context.

Other researchers have used field studies where they utilized log files and supplemented these with interviews and focus groups. In some cases, the studies are of short duration. For example, Oulasvirta et al. [158] paired various mobile situations (i.e., waiting for a subway, having coffee with someone, moving through a busy street, traveling on a bus or subway, standing in a busy commuting spot, or sitting in a laboratory) with various web search tasks in an experimental study that lasted approximately an hour and a half. Göker & Myrhaugb [64] also performed a field experiment of this nature where participants were assigned information seeking tasks as they wandered in an outdoor tourist area. In contrast, Rahamti & Zhong [168] conducted a four-month field study where they combined data logs with focus group interviews. The analysis of such studies has focused on the question of interest (for example, cognitive resources used to complete mobile tasks in various physical environments [158]), but in general these log studies have documented mobile interaction by category e.g., social networking, news, games, etc.

Collectively, these studies have contributed an understanding of mobile use in everyday life, and the factors that influence its adoption and use. Firstly, mobile diary studies have shown that mobile use is heavily context dependent [106]. Context may be taken to mean physical location or social setting [20, 39]. Users favor mobile devices for the convenience they afford and their ability to integrate the device into everyday life activities, including social interactions [39, 40, 193]. In instances where researchers have been motivated to examine information interactions on mobile devices, context has been shown to influence users' information needs and the perceived relevance of the information they locate [64]. Context also influences time. Studies have emphasized that people are using their mobiles under time constraints or to pass time, depending on the circumstances [40, 196]. Secondly, mobile devices must have functional affordances [39, 40], yet early concerns about the usability of the device (i.e., small screens) seem to be waning. Nylander, for example, found that people preferred to use mobile phones even when they had access to a desktop and laptop computer [146]. Lastly, mobile user experience studies have raised important questions about the nature of attention. Due to the ubiquity of the technology, total absorption in the mobile device is not optimal in terms of safety. Mobile users must shift their attention between the device and the external environment [158], yet some research has noted the "habit-forming" nature of mobiles [157].

Another approach to understanding user attitudes toward mobiles has been to use questionnaires. Wakefield & Whitten [201] designed a study situated in a classroom environment where university students were shown an image of a Blackberry PDA on a large screen and given further information on either the function of hedonic uses and specifications of the Blackberry. They were then asked to complete a questionnaire that included items on the perceived ease of use and use of the device, its playfulness, whether they found it to be cognitively absorbing and enjoyable, and their behavioral intentions. They found that whether participants were presented with the hedonic or utilitarian specifications and uses of the device influenced their perceptions and intentions to use the device. For example, those in the hedonic condition believed the Blackberry valued playfulness and were more likely to judge the PDA as enjoyable and useful and say they intended to use it.

Rather than analyze mobile experiences, Kim et al. [102] employed a different strategy to understand mobile user engagement. They performed content and feature analysis of over 100 branded mobile apps selected from free apps representing sixty-eight companies sourced through the 2010 Interbrand Global Brands and the iTunes store. Branded mobile apps were those that prominently displayed a brand name, logo or icon. Based on previous literature, they proposed that the following characteristics of mobile apps would be important for user engagement: vividness, novelty, motivation, control, customization, feedback, and multiplatforming. They found that almost all of the apps examined incorporated at least one of these seven characteristics: control (97.2%), customization (85.8%), vividness (78.3%: entire app, 86.8%: entry page), multiplatforming (70.8%), motivation (62.3%), feedback (55.7%), and novelty (11.3%). Some observations made in their analysis were that branded apps tended to try to foster user engagement through the inclusion of recommendations and customization (e.g., "my store") based on saving users' personal information or determining their geographical location. They also noted that vividness was typically operationalized using images, and that apps made it possible for users to share information via and connect to social networking sites.

Recently, Lagun et al. [109] looked at one component of user engagement, user attention, on search results in the mobile context. Web search has seen a rapid growth in mobile search traffic, and an increasing trend toward providing answer-like results (e.g., weather, stock price, world-cup fixtures and results). Such results display the answer on the search result page itself. As a consequence, and as expected, clicks on the results are often rare, making it challenging to evaluate their quality. Motivated by this and work on mouse tracking in search (Section 3.4.2), Lagun et al. studied whether tracking the browser viewport, which is the visible portion of a webpage, on mobiles could enable accurate measurement of user attention, and provide good measurement of search satisfaction in the absence of clicks. They designed a lab study where they varied the answer presence and relevance to a user's information need. They elicited satisfaction ratings on the result relevance from the users, and recorded both gaze and viewport data as users performed search tasks. They saw that an increased scrolling past an answer and an increased time below an answer are strong—and measurable signals—of user dissatisfaction with the answers. They also found strong correlations between gaze duration and viewport duration. This work suggests that viewport may be used as scale to provide reliable signals on how satisfied users are with answer-like results, and what users are focusing on while inspecting the result list. The application of this technology and associated signals in user engagement measurement looks promising.

In summary, work in the area of mobile user engagement will continue to gain momentum, and will be most successful through a combination of quantitative and qualitative approaches that address what activities users are carrying out on their mobile devices, but also what is their motivation and subjective evaluation of the experience. In a recent study of mobile information interactions, O'Brien & Absar [2] used diaries and interviews to test a model of user engagement that included the attributes of usability, aesthetic appeal, novelty, felt involvement, attention, endurability, time, and context. Given the emphasis on the importance of context in the user experience literature, they asked participants to take a photo of the physical setting in which the information interaction took place. These visual pieces of data are being analyzed to determine if there are characteristics of mobile user environments that are essential to user engagement, but not accessible through log files or diary entries. Future research may also employ physiological measures on a larger scale to examine the users' levels of arousal during mobile interactions, or participant observation to gauge the users' mobile environment, e.g., degree of social interaction, general distractions, etc.

5.4   SUMMARY

In summary, this chapter has explored three scenarios that take us beyond the single site, single task scenario of web desktop use. First, we discussed the concept of multitasking, a behavior that more closely approximates real-world behavior. While information retrieval research has studied multitasking over the last decade, only recently have we made an implicit link between user engagement and multitasking. The work of Lehmann et al. proposed two new metrics, cumulative activity and activity pattern, derived from analytic data, to explore and explain the complex relationship between users' behavioral engagement with websites based on their time on and away from websites, and their activities upon revisiting websites. Second, networked user engagement speaks to the desire to keep users engaged with content providers, and examines the relationship between the goal-orientation of websites and user engagement as measured by dwell time, linking, and downstream engagement metrics. Both multitasking and multi-site engagement utilize analytic measures in new ways to study more complex phenomena associated with web engagement (Chapter 4).

Yet we know that online browsing—irrespective of the number of tasks performed or sites visited—is increasingly taking place on mobile devices. Thus we also provided some synthesis of work in the area of user experience of how users engage with their mobile devices (based on diary, interview and log studies), and how mobile apps meet engagement criteria.

All of the scenarios discussed in this chapter demonstrate that, while we might reduce the study of user engagement to a single site and single task for simplicity's sake, we must also build a more realistic picture of engagement based on how online browsing occurs in the real world. Single site, single session desktop studies are necessary for building the foundations of measurement, and as we become more confident in the reliability and validity of self-report, analytic, and physiological measures as indicators of user engagement, we can begin to construct more complex usage scenarios and consider how to appropriately apply various methodologies. This may mean utilizing existing measures in new ways, or creating new measures, for example, downstream engagement and cumulative activity, or looking more closely at how users' social and physical contexts—as in the case of mobile engagement—affects our choice of measures. Ultimately, as we learn more about the phenomena of user engagement and its measurement, we will be better equipped to tackle the ubiquitous and multifaceted computing environment.

CHAPTER 6

Enhancing the Rigor of User Engagement Methods and Measures

Previous chapters reported on the use of self-report, analytic, and physiological methods, and highlighted the benefits and drawbacks of each approach for measuring user engagement. We also discussed emerging work in the areas of multitasking, mobile use, and networked engagement that are challenging us to move beyond the single task, single website, desktop model of user engagement. This presentation has allowed us to address current methodological and measurement practices—and the research that has applied them—in great depth, but is limited in that we have thus far examined them in isolation. The reason for this is that, as we have demonstrated, the measurement of an experiential concept such as engagement is complex. Multiple user attributes, e.g., motivation and attention, and system attributes, e.g., aesthetic appeal, novelty, and interactivity, coalesce to create, shape, and predict online interactions.

Mixed methods are a means of capturing this complexity. In some cases, factors such as scale and setting inhibit the use of multiple methods. For example, it is impossible to collect large-scale analytic data concurrently with self-report and physiological data from the remote browsing sessions of millions of users. Another issue, however, is the appropriateness of the measures selected to examine user engagement in a given context, and this requires us to critically evaluate the tools of data collection and analysis that we use, both alone and in concert. In other words, we need to have reliable and valid individual measures and methods to evaluate user engagement, and these methods and measures should corroborate each other when used collectively in a research study. Thus, it is not only about measuring user engagement, but critically assessing how we do so.

In Section 1.4, we introduced five dimensions: scale, setting, temporality; objectivity/subjectivity; and process-/product-based methods and measures. We used these dimensions throughout this book to highlight the types of trade-offs that take place in studies. For example, we discussed both large-scale, behavior-based metrics (i.e., web analytics) gathered "in the wild," and small-scale laboratory-based work that used eye tracking or think-after protocols to capture physiological and perceptual responses to an experience. In this chapter, we recast these five dimensions not as trade-offs, but as opportunities to advance the measurement of user engagement.

The aim of this chapter is to revisit the dimensions of scale, setting, temporality, objectivity/subjectivity, and process-/product-based measurement. The intention here is to demonstrate that each of these dimensions are not binary, but operate along a continuum; effective research designs can employ methods and measures along the continuum in concert or iteratively to contribute more meaningfully to the study of user engagement. We draw upon published work and our own experiences to report on the use of mixed methods work and discuss the need for more research of this kind.

6.1   SCALE

Scale refers to the size of a sampled population participating in a study. This may range from a dozen people participating in a qualitative or physiological study, to hundreds of online survey respondents, to millions of user actions documented through web analytics. Small-scale measurements are deep and rich, but limited in terms of generalizability, whereas large-scale measurements are powerful but are hard to account for users' motivation and context. Obviously, the choice of scale will often be dictated by the availability of resources and expertise, and the scope of the study.

Large-scale data collection methods have been used within the web analytics community and by Internet marketing research companies (e.g., comScore)[1] for many years. Due to the scale of these studies (i.e., millions of users), measures collected are used as proxies of user engagement with the assumption that greater activity and frequency of use equates with higher engagement. Although these studies cannot explicitly explain why users engage with a site, patterns of interaction capture from such a large sample of users provide a strong indication of "site engagement" or so-called "stickiness." By varying specific aspects of the site, e.g., structure, layout and functionality, and assessing the effect of these on online behavior, web analytics can provide implicit understanding on why users engage with the site. For instance, a known strategy to keep users interacting with a news site is to provide links at various positions and of various types (e.g., "related stories," "other big news," and "editor picks") on its pages, enticing users to consume more content, thus staying longer on the news site and increasing its "stickiness." However, even if a successful strategy is found to encourage stickiness, understanding its impact remains largely superficial and may not go beyond usability and functionality issues. In addition, the strategy may only work short-term with no clear reasons as to why.

Small-scale measurements potentially bring deeper insights. Returning to the example of a news site, the click-through rate on a particular link may be very low. Could this be due to its position, its type, or the anchor text? Several online experiments could be carried out (e.g., through A/B testing) to provide answers. Yet there could be another explanation for the low click-through rate. For instance, if the link is always coupled with flickering images, or the content disinterests the user, then the user will not be enticed to click-through. Other web analytics measures may help make sense of such interactions (for example, examining dwell time on the page, an indication of user interest in the content, in conjunction with the link click-through rate), but to a limited extent. A small-scale experiment could have identified the problem more readily and with fewer

---

[1]http://www.comscore.com.

participants; for example an eye tracking study may show that users became distracted by the flickering images and did not attend to the link.

Small-scale studies that utilize eye tracking have been very successful at identifying where users focus on the interface. By designing careful experiments, it is possible to relate what the user is focusing on and why the eyes are being drawn to these areas of interest on the screen (e.g., relevant versus non-relevant results on a search engine result page, headlines in a particular font, flickering images at fixed versus varying positions). Recently, Gwizdka [71] used eye tracking to derive cognitive effort measures and examined these with respect to document relevance and perceived relevance. Results demonstrated different reading patterns according to the relevance of documents (task relevant, irrelevant, topically—though not task—relevant), and that mental workload was highest for topically relevant documents, but similar for task relevant and irrelevant documents, due to the level of decision making required to determine utility. This work is promising for the study of user engagement, since cognitive load may be an important predictor of overall user experience if we return to the idea of "challenge" and the need to stimulate but not overwhelm users as they navigate and interact with web spaces (see Richness and Control, an important characteristic of user engagement, discussed in Section 1.3.6).

It is interesting to note that, although Gwizdka recruited only twenty-four people for the above experiment, each individual completed twenty-one trials of two task types (targeted word search and constricted information search) [71]. By designing the experiment with brief tasks that required a binary "yes" or "no" response to whether or not the viewed news stories were relevant, Gwizdka generated sufficient data for classifying, aggregating, and analyzing eye movement and pupil dilation data. This is a useful example of how we can play with scale in an experimental study to generate reliable and meaningful results.

Another example of this is the recent work of Arapakis et al. [11], who used eye tracking and self-reported focused attention and affect to explore the role of interestingness in user engagement. They used a large-scale linguistic technique—sentiment analysis—to construct a corpus of eighteen news articles from over 13,000 items in a news portal that varied in interestingness and polarity. These news items were then utilized in an experimental study to demonstrate that eye tracking metrics (e.g., time to first fixation, duration of fixation, etc.) differed across news articles of varying interestingness. Participants spent significantly more time browsing and gazed longer at the titles of interesting articles; interesting articles also generated more frequent, rapid, and prolonged fixations. The eye tracking data corroborated with results of the focused attention and affect questionnaires. This study confirmed the fundamental role of user interest in promoting engagement. While this may seem like an obvious outcome, a major contribution of this study was the alignment of the physiological and two self-report measures in the assessment of interest in news articles. Interestingness is a crucial component of user engagement—particularly for capturing and sustaining user engagement. Future work should look at how these measures align with respect to other aspects of the reading experience. In fact, Arapakis et al. [11] already showed in the same work that the eye tracking and affect measures were in agreement based on the sentimentality of the articles.[2]

The above study is particular useful because the authors mapped self-report and eye tracking measures to mouse tracking, as reported in [9]. In Section 3.4, we discussed the relationship between eye tracking and cursor tracking in greater depth. In this instance [9], the authors recorded mouse movements, from which they generated mouse gesture patterns. Through the use of unsupervised learning, they built a taxonomy of cursor patterns that shared similar properties. These gestures were generated independent of page layout, the type of element contained, or relative position, making this methodology applicable to other contexts. Furthermore, the authors identified several significant correlations between cursor behavior and focused attention and affect. More specifically, they noticed that certain types of mouse gestures were negatively correlated with focused attention, and that negative emotions were more influential on cursor behavior than positive ones. In fact, these correlations were more pronounced than those with gaze movement. This observation is consistent with previous work [38, 142] showing that mouse-related signals are sensitive to frustrating and unpleasant experiences, and task difficulty.

This is important because, if eye tracking is a reliable indicator of interestingness and correlates with self-reported focused attention and affect, then the alignment between eye tracking and cursor movement (which is scalable) shows promise for connecting small- and large-scale measurements. Millions of users interact daily with online applications without providing any explicit feedback about the quality of their experience. Therefore, any effort toward developing a more nuanced understanding of user online behavior is important to understand the quality and level of engagement. Mouse tracking may be able to address this need in a low-cost and scalable manner without removing users from their natural setting. Overall, the message of the study was "that engagement manifests in different forms such as the gaze behavior of users that develop an emotional, cognitive, and behavioral connection with a digital resource (e.g., an interesting news article), but also as observable and distinct mouse cursor patterns" [9]. A logical next step would be to relate mouse patterns to web analytics metrics, both at inter- and intra-session levels. Looking at these will be particularly useful with mobile devices; see [109] for some initial investigations.

6.2   SETTING

Data collection may take place in the laboratory or "in the wild." A laboratory setting may be necessary to observe behaviors directly, particularly if eye tracking or physiological sensors are utilized to record this behavior. It also facilitates a higher level of consistency and control, which enhances the internal validity of the measurement. Internal validity may be especially important in the context of user engagement, where method and measures continue to emerge and evolve.

---

[2]The sentimentality expressed in the news articles was calculated using SentiStrength, a widely used lexicon-based, sentiment analysis tool [194].

Laboratory settings are essential for evaluating the effects of new design functionalities, or isolating specific components of the user interaction.

Measurements conducted "in the wild" or field have greater external validity and are more "true to life." Examples range from collecting and analyzing log file data to conducting ethnographic research in participants' homes or workplaces. Log analysis can be performed on a larger scale through web analytics, or on a smaller scale, for instance, as part of a longitudinal study. Log analysis can be used to track more naturalistic behaviors if installed on people's own devices and with consent. Another advantage is that during the study, it is possible to prompt the user at intervals or daily to review and annotate their behaviors to add more explanation to them [95].

A setting that stands between laboratory and "in the wild" is crowd-sourcing [129]. Crowd-sourcing is the "process of obtaining needed services, ideas, or content by soliciting contributions from a large group of people, and especially from an online community, rather than from traditional employees or suppliers."[3] A well known crowd-sourcing platform is Amazon Mechanical Turk[4] (AMT).

Crowd-sourcing combines several benefits for running online experiments, as recently stated in [12]. Firstly, researchers have access to a large pool of participants with fairly stable availability over time. The diversity of participants' background in terms of age, ethnicity, and socio-economic status is something that is very difficult to reach in typical laboratory setting. Crowd-sourcing experiments such as those on AMT can be conducted at a much lower cost than laboratory ones. Finally, they can be used to conduct medium- to large-scale, labor-intensive study under strict time constraints. However, they possess several limitations such as threats to ecological validity, lack of control over the experimental setting, distractions in the physical environment, anonymity of participants. Particular to this setting, is the importance in taking preventive measures to discount low-quality responses and undesirable participants, for example, using validation tests and strict selection criteria. On this aspect, see [130] for a study about pay incentives and quality of AMT responses, and [50] for using gamification in crowd-sourced relevance assessments in information retrieval.

Crowd-sourcing was used by McCay-Peet et al. [134] to study the impact of saliency of task-relevant information on two engagement metrics, focused attention and affect (we briefly discussed this work already in Section 2.6.3). Around 200 participants were recruited via AMT to respond to an online survey that included information-seeking tasks; half were provided with webpages where the task-related headlines were salient while the other half were given webpages where the headlines were not salient. The results showed that saliency affected affect, mostly that a drop of affect was observed in the non-salient case. No effect was observed with respect to focus attention, although users reported in the open-ended questions that it was easier to focus in the salient condition. Interestingly, user interest in webpage content was found to be a good predictor

---

[3]http://en.wikipedia.org/wiki/Crowdsourcing.
[4]https://www.mturk.com/mturk/.

of focused attention, which in turn was a good predictor of positive affect. This again highlights the fundamental role of interestingness in promoting an engaging experience.

What this study showed is that using crowd-sourcing was an effective way to conduct a study to investigate user engagement. While the use of AMT as a platform for online recruitment reduces the environmental control of a laboratory setting (e.g., control over screen size, Internet connection speed), it also allows for more rapid testing and a larger and more diverse participant base than the average user study. In addition, as stated by the authors themselves [134], the AMT participants provided excellent responses to open-ended questions, which were both thoughtful and contributed significantly to the interpretation of the results. This further demonstrates the viability of this setting to carry out user engagement studies.

6.3   TEMPORALITY

Temporality refers to the duration of user engagement, in terms of whether it is a short-term "snapshot" or a more long-term examination of the user experience. In both cases, we must consider whether the timeframe is capturing single individuals in one or multiple sessions, or all activity on a particular website within a period of a few hours or several weeks. In other words, the user, the web application, or both may be the unit of analysis.

Web analytics (Chapter 4) allow behavioral engagement to be tracked daily, weekly, monthly, etc. For instance dwell time and click-through rates, two intra-session metrics, can be tracked so that any fluctuations can be identified and acted upon. They do not look at each user, but at "the users" in total. By contrast, inter-session metrics focus on "each user" and their long-term value. It is important to relate intra- and inter-session metrics for the purposes of relating short-term engagement (e.g., time spent on a site) to long-term engagement (e.g., return rate). This will facilitate understanding of how to keep users satisfied and thus engaged (e.g., returning sooner than later). Several inter-session metrics were discussed in Section 4.5; here, as an illustration, we focus on one of them, absence time, which was described in Section 4.5.3. The hypothesis is that engaged users come back sooner, and hence their absence times are shorter. Can we predict the absence time based on intra-session metrics?

Using survival analysis [1], Dupret & Lalmas [48] explored the relationship between absence time and various intra-session engagement (search) metrics such as abandonment rates, clickthrough rates, and number of views. For example, they saw that while observing a click was, on average, better than observing no click, a click at the first position of the ranking was a weaker indicator of success than a click at the third position. This in itself is not new as many search evaluation methodologies account for this. They also found that, on average, clicks after the fifth positions reflected a poorer user experience; users cannot find the information they are looking for. Clicking lower in the ranking suggested a more careful choice from the user, while clicking at the bottom was a sign that the overall ranking was of low quality. Users who find their answers quickly returned sooner to the search application. While these experiments were carried in the context of a search tool on a questioning & answering system, they are representative of the results that could be reached for other ranking applications.

Using absence time as the inter-session metric of user engagement to "optimize for," made the interpretation of the click behaviors possible. From these, the search tool can now look at optimizing several search metrics, with the knowledge of what this would mean in terms of long-term user engagement. Survival Analysis takes a longitudinal view of the data, and with it, it was possible to relate the experience of individual users and their activity on a search site to their absence time. This was done at a more fined-grained level, without sacrificing the large-scale character of the analysis that is possible with the record of users' online behavior [48].

Multitasking and networked user engagement measures are also concerned with the temporality of engagement. Both account for the fact that users access a site several times during their online sessions, and that several sites are accessed within a same session. Sections 5.1 and 5.2 presented several such measures. Recent work following this line is that of [120] who use metrics borrowed from complex network analysis area [145] to measure networked user engagement. Sites were modeled as nodes whereas the traffic between sites constituted edges, weighted by the volume of the traffic between the two sites. Several such networks could be formed, for instance accounting for the different types of user loyalty, countries, weekday versus weekend. They observed that, for instance, very loyal users access more sites and navigate more between them, leaving a network of sites does not mean less engagement, and finally user traffic varies across countries. The types of sites being accessed differed between weekdays and weekend. The temporal dimension is with respect to the session; the metrics are concerned with measuring user engagement at session-level instead of site-level. The next step would be to see how these metrics could be used in tandem with inter-session metrics, as was done in [48] who related absence time (an inter-session metric) with search (intra-session) engagement metrics.

So far, we have discussed the temporality dimension in the context of large-scale measurement, mainly web analytics. It is important to also carry out longitudinal small-scale measurement of user engagement. Longitudinal research is a type of method used to discover relationships between variables that are not related to various background variables. It may involve studying the same group of individuals over an extended period of time. Data is first collected at the outset of the study, and may then be gathered repeatedly throughout the length of the study. The benefit of this type of research is that it allows for assessing changes over time, and as such are typically used in the social sciences to examine lifespan and development issues, and in healthcare to look at, for instance, risk factors for disease. In the case of user engagement, we may want to understand how users' perceptions of online systems evolve over time, as they gain increased efficacy and familiarity with an application.

Cross-sectional research is related to longitudinal research, but involves looking at different groups of people (males and females, experts and novices) at a particular point in time. This type of work may be especially useful for exploring the role of individual differences on user engagement. The caveat of both longitudinal and cross-sectional designs is that they are, in their strictest definition, observational, and the environment must not be manipulated in any way. Thus performing longitudinal work may be complicated by the rapid rate of change in information technology, and we would need to account for the introduction of new interfaces, devices, versions, etc., in long-term observations.

There is however not enough longitudinal work in user engagement studies. One reason is the resource intensiveness of such designs; longitudinal methods take time, and therefore, do not produce "quick" results. This is problematic from an academic and industry standpoint where there is often a race to produce papers and introduce new products to the marketplace. In addition to the time issue, longitudinal methods are often quite expensive; funding opportunities for academic researchers occur in short cycles (i.e., a few years). Lastly, longitudinal studies often have only a small group of subjects, which makes it difficult to apply the results to a larger population. Another problem is that participants sometimes drop out of the study, shrinking the sample size and decreasing the amount of data collected.

Despite the drawbacks, there is currently a great deal of interest in longitudinal work. For example, Karapanos et al. [93] led a workshop on the topic at the Computing and Human Factors (CHI) conference in 2012 where they invited researchers to engage with them around issues of "Theories, Methods, and Case Studies of Longitudinal Research." This workshop was one of many events dating back to 2007 that this group organized annually at CHI. In their workshop position paper, the authors pointed to the number of emerging theories of user experience and product adoption with a temporal element, popularity of psychology-based methods for gathering longitudinal data (e.g., Experience Sampling Method [114]), and the burgeoning number of technologies across domain areas that would benefit from such work.

Karapanos et al.'s prioritization for longitudinal research in User Experience is equally applicable to user engagement [93]: "The more ambitious the planned impact of interactive products on people's experiences and social practices, the stronger the need to study consequences of product use over longer periods of time." We have highlighted the idea of tracking experiences throughout this discussion, but have not addressed "social practices," which opens up broader questions about how engaging with technologies impacts individuals and society in terms of its interference and/or harmony with daily lives and routines. We cannot find such answers by limiting our studies to laboratory-based settings and momentary snapshots into people's interactions with the web. We need more longitudinal study designs that are appropriate to study user engagement in a way that can lead to insights that are meaningful and actionable. However, we must also address methodological issues associated with their use: What are the right trade-offs in terms of how often to observe people, which ethnographic methods to use, how to extend the window of analysis for analytical data in a meaningful manner (for example to compare different days of the week, months, etc., over a year period). More research is needed to identify viable methodologies applicable to the measurement of user engagement.

6.4   OBJECTIVITY AND SUBJECTIVITY

Measures of user engagement can be described as subjective or objective. Subjective measures record users' self-reported perceptions of the online experience at hand. As discussed in Chapter 2 self-reports in the form of interviews, questionnaires, and think-aloud protocols are commonly used to study user engagement, and these methods have been used in concert to define user engagement and criteria for its measurement. For instance, [150] reported a literature review and exploratory interview study with users in four domains (online shopping, web searching, educational webcasting, video games), which led to the identification of a set of user engagement attributes. This was then used to develop a questionnaire to assess user engagement, which was evaluated in two large-scale online studies, leading to the widely used User Engagement Scale questionnaire (UES) described in Section 2.6.3. In Chapter 2 we relayed the benefits and drawbacks of subjective measures: the ability to capture users' experiences in their own words versus the challenges associated with post-hoc interpretation and the halo effect [180].

A common strategy to overcome the challenges of subjective measures is to use objective measures that can reliably indicate subjective states [84], albeit raising the question of what objective phenomena are indicative of engagement (we return to this later but see [176] for a proposal to map large-scale user-centered metrics to product goals). Examples of objective measures include follow-on task performance, user physiology (e.g., arousal, heart rate) and activity (e.g., mouse tracking) and eye tracking—see Chapter 3. With the exception of mouse tracking (see Section 3.4), these measures, although objective, are suitable for measuring only a small number of interaction episodes with proximal users.

Another group of objective measures of engagement are online behavior metrics, i.e., web analytics metrics, that aim at assessing users' depth of engagement with a site. Widely used metrics include click-through rates, number of page views, time spent on a site (dwell time), how often users return to a site and number of users per month. Dwell time has proven to be a meaningful and robust metric of user engagement over the years; for example in the context of web search [88] where it is used to improve retrieval [5, 24], and recently in personalized-based ranking tasks [210].

Web analytics metrics may be objective measures, but their interpretations may not always be straightforward (e.g., more time spent on a page may not always imply greater interest in its content). In recent work [112], dwell time was used as proxy of user satisfaction on landing pages of mobile advertisements: higher dwell times were observed when the landing pages were not mobile optimized, compared to those that were. Using this signal blindly in an ad-serving algorithm would mean promoting advertisements with non-mobile-optimized landing pages, which obviously is wrong in terms of the long-term value perspective and for user engagement. The authors found that this counterintuitive result could be explained by the fact that with some non-optimized landing pages, users tried to understand what the ad was about, before decided to leave the page; decision making was quicker on mobile-optimized landing pages.

The most optimal situation is when we can use subjective and objective measures in concert and with confidence that they corroborate our findings. Examples of using combinations of subjective and objective measures have been previously discussed in this chapter in terms of scale (see Section 6.1). The works of [11] and [9] showed alignment between self-reported focused attention and affect, eye tracking, and cursor movements in the context of interestingness and a news reading experience. The experience was, however, static: users were shown webpages (e.g., news articles) and their engagement was measured during this exposure.

To extend these findings to the "live" web, Warnock & Lalmas [203] recruited participants from AMT but asked them to complete reading and fact-finding tasks on live websites, thereby allowing them to engage more naturally with website content using their own hardware in their natural environment. Around 350 participants were tracked as they used modified variants of a news website,[5] a normal and an "ugly" version (Figure 6.4). A detailed questionnaire was administered to obtain self-reported focused attention and affect (as in [134]), but also other self-report measures such as aesthetics and interestingness (the authors adapted the User Engagement Scale described in 2.6.3). Mouse movements were recorded and translated into metrics such as movement speed, click rate, pause length. The study therefore employed several subjective measures and one objective measure.

The researchers found differences in cursor movements by task type (fact-finding versus reading) which is to be expected. With regard to self-reported aesthetics, the "ugly" variant of the site did not, surprisingly, result in lower aesthetics scores. This finding was made even more unusual when participant comments were taken into consideration: "The font and the colors used were really distracting to me"; "Multiple font colors within the same page = hard to read." Participants were not prompted to discuss the interface in any way, yet a large number of participants left negative comments about the "ugly" version of the interface. These comments suggest that the aesthetics scores did not accurately reflect the aesthetics of the interface. There were also no significant correlations between any of the cursor metrics and the other subjective measures, even when the interestingness of the task was taken into account. However, interestingness was found to influence affect and focused attention, thus further confirming this relationship [9, 11, 134].

How do we explain these findings? While it is possible that participants might have randomly clicked through the survey, this was not the case; the manual result verification showed that all questions were answered to a high standard, and the majority of participants took extra time to answer optional parts of the questionnaire.

There could be several reasons for these negative results (beyond the typical drawbacks associated with using questionnaires such as the inflation of ratings [99]—see Section 2.5): a flawed methodology, a non-existent signal, or the wrong measure. In terms of the methodology, due to between-groups design of the experiment, participants had no basis of comparison for the engagement metrics, which could have impacted their answers. However, performing a within-subject study where participants interacted with two variances of the website would have potentially in-

---

[5]The study was also carried out on Wikipedia, and the same results were obtained.

Figure 6.1: Comparison of normal webpages with the "ugly" variants (the site was BBC News). The latter were modified by changing the colors to create a high contrast, changing the fonts to Comic Sans and Impact, the injection of advertising banners and the obfuscation of navigation elements. Taken from [203].

troduced confounds and not addressed their engagement with the website. It could also be that the experience induced by the "ugly" version of the interface was not negative enough for users to become annoyed, and thus down-marking it. However experimenting with an uglier interface is not right (unless the aim is to test this hypothesis) as measuring user engagement makes sense only if the experience is in principle positive. Although usability is an important characteristic of user engagement, *usability issues* must be fixed first before thinking about user engagement measurements. Another possible source for interference is the Hawthorne effect [132]; participants were notified that their cursor was being tracked, which could have influenced both their cursor movements and the engagement measures.

In hindsight, this study demonstrates several things. Again carrying out user engagement studies using crowd-sourcing works. Designing experiments to obtain reliable insights about user engagement and its measurement remains nonetheless challenging. Finally, not finding a signal may simply mean that some of the metrics used were not the correct ones.

Indeed, the results reported in [203] suggest there is no relationship between the metrics used to represent the cursor movement and engagement measures. Yet these metrics represent only a fraction of the data that can be extracted from the cursor behavior. As suggested by the authors themselves, one approach might be to apply statistical clustering methods to reveal specific types of movement in the same way that gaze tracking studies observe saccades and fixations. This is in fact what Arapakis et al. in their latest work [9] did, which was shown to correlate with subjective engagement metrics, namely focus attention and affect (see Section 6.1).

However, O'Brien & Lebow [149] found that the relationship between subjective and objective measures is not straightforward. This study was also situated in the online news domain and asked participants to browse a news website guided by a social information-seeking scenario. Self-report measures, namely the UES, System Usability Scale [28], and Cognitive Absorption Scale [4] were highly correlated with each other and users' assessment of the interestingness of the material they examined. However, there was no significant difference in the reading times, browsing times, overall time, and numbers of pages visited by people in the low, medium, and high engagement group (as measured by the UES); physiological differences also did not differ significantly. One issue was that, due to the sample size of 30, the UES was not examined according to its sub-scales, and it is possible that an overall score masked differences that may have been present within the sub-scales. However, there was a relationship between electrodermal activity (see Section 3.1), and interestingness, and those who experienced low and high cognitive absorption spent significantly more time reading, browsing, and overall; low cognitive absorption was also associated with a higher number of pages visited. Thus, there was some corroboration between some of the subjective and objective measures, but the authors indicated that further research into the reliability and validity of each of these, and more mixed methods work to examine their relationship was necessary.

6.5   PROCESS- AND PRODUCT-BASED

When measuring user engagement, we may be interested to asses how users engage with a particular product, such as a news website or an email tool. We might use a questionnaire or calculate the total number of clicks, and dwell time. By examining people's overall perceptions of a product, or aggregated analytic data, we gain an understanding of their experience in their own words, or are able to compare web applications on various measures. However, we do not have the fine-grained analysis of the moment-by-moment interactions between user and system. Thus, we distinguish product-based measures and process-based measures. While the former gives important insights regarding users' overall level of engagement with an online application, and the ability to compare to others, the latter may show us what aspects of the interaction were particularly engaging or disengaging.

In the case of product-based measures, we must be careful in our interpretation of the indicators we use for user engagement, and their long-term significance. A website perceived as more aesthetically pleasing than another may be less engaging; a beautiful website may not promote an experience that users want to repeat or feel particularly drawn into. A website for which the average dwell time is higher than another may also not translate in better long-term engagement. Thus multiple product measures that address different attributes of engagement are needed to make sense of the user experience.

In the case of process-based measures, data points are collected over time. For example, we might be interested in how individual electrodermal activity (an indicator of physiological arousal) changes over the course of interacting with a news website when viewing positive and negative content; the work on eye tracking and document relevance discussed earlier [71] is a good example of work being done in this area. However, it highlights the care that must be taken to clean and process the data, including syncing multiple data streams. We need to know, for example, what document was being examined at what point in time that generated a particular neurophysiological response. With process-based measures, the intention is to discover where a behavioral, cognitive, or affective change occurred during the course of interacting with an application.

Process-based measurement is particularly important nowadays because users engage heavily in multitasking (see Section 5.1). In [121], several metrics based on web analytics were defined to account for the multitasking effect. For instance, they found that time spent on social media sites increased for each revisit, whereas the opposite was observed for email sites. A possible explanation is that, for email sites, there are less messages to read in subsequent visits, whereas for social media sites, users have more time to spend as other tasks are completed over the course of the online session. These metrics are instances of process-based measurement; they looking at user engagement with a site across the whole session, and not just with respect to individual visits to the site. In the context of networked user engagement, process-based measurement makes even more sense as users are visiting sites from the same Internet service provider. The sites may not be the same (news versus email sites), but there will be high connectivity between them in terms of look and feel, branding, and hyperlinking. The downstream engagement measure presented in Section 5.2 and the metrics based on complex network analysis area proposed in [120] (see Section 6.3) are examples of process-based measurement. They look at the process of engagement with a network of sites offered by a same large company.

One challenge for the measure of user engagement is to corroborate product- and process-based measures. Similar to our argument for increased use of mixed methods and greater correspondence between subjective and objective measures, our ability to collect and make sense of product- and process-based measures simultaneously will advance the area of measurement. In addition, this discussion of product- and process-based measured overlaps with the temporal characteristics previously examined, as we need reliable methods for identifying what is occurring within participants and/or system interactions, when it is occurring, and how this contributes to an overall picture of user engagement.

6.6 SUMMARY

This chapter provides our views of measurement challenges and opportunities based on our own work and experiences, and our understanding of current practices and research. We presented this chapter according to the five dimensions of user engagement measurement, postulated in Section 1.4: scale, setting, temporality, objectivity and subjectivity, and process- and product-based measures. A particular focus throughout was the usage of mixed methods, which have started to appear, and are helping to build more valid and reliable user engagement methodologies and measures, with the aim to increase our confidence in interpreting measurement outcomes.

We end this chapter with a gentle warning. Today, an online application may be very engaging (popular, well recommended within the user community, acclaimed for its design or functionality served, etc.); it may become less so in future. The reason may have little to do with the online application, but more with the fashion of the moment. What makes an engaging experience today may not work tomorrow. Users change, needs change, and trends change, some quicker than others. Disruptive technologies may also bring a totally new ecosystem, eventually redefining what engagement means and how it is measured.

CHAPTER 7

Conclusions and Future Research Directions

This chapter summarizes the methods and measures presented in this book, discusses future research directions, and concludes with our main "take-away" messages.

7.1 SUMMARY

User engagement is the quality of the user experience that emphasizes the positive aspect of interacting with an online application, where users want to use that application longer and repeatedly. Nowadays, users invest time, attention, and emotion in their use of technology. Thus, there is an impetus to move beyond ensuring applications are merely usable, and to consider the hedonic and experiential factors of interacting with technology, such as fun, fulfillment, play, and user engagement. Measurement is critical for evaluating whether applications successfully engage users.

In Chapter 1, we introduced the focus of this book, defined user engagement and listed its main characteristics, as reported in the literature. We adopted the broad definition from Attfield et al. [15], which identified emotional, cognitive, and behavioral factors of user engagement. This definition also ensured that we referred equally to user engagement in terms of a single session or across multiple sessions. The latter was shown to be particularly important in Chapter 4, when approaches on web analytics were presented. The chapter also introduced the concept of subjectivity, scale, temporality, setting, and process and product, important factors to account for in the design and evaluation of measurement approaches.

User engagement is a multifaceted, complex phenomenon, which makes it a particularly challenging construct to measure. We addressed three main measurement approaches, self-report, physiological, and web analytics, that are currently being employed. Each is described in a separate chapter, from Chapter 2 to Chapter 4, respectively.

Chapter 2 explored self-report measures of user engagement, namely interviews, think aloud/think after protocols, and questionnaires. We began by providing an overview of general considerations for using self-report methods, and then addressed interviews, think aloud/think after protocols, and questionnaires in more detail, illustrating each with concrete examples from user engagement studies. Particularly useful is the list of user engagement questionnaires that have been developed and validated. Many of these have been used in recent work, both in their entirety and more piece-meal, depending on the domain of interest, and the constraints and goals of the study.

Chapter 3 reported techniques based on physiological measurement. We first described a subset of physiological measures, referred to as psychophysiological measures, which includes measures of bodily and brain response and functioning. We then discussed the use of eye tracking, mouse tracking, and cameras for recording user behavior. A large part of this chapter was dedicated to eye tracking and cursor tracking because of extensive investigations that use these as a measurement tool and discuss their potential (in particular mouse tracking) in the study of user engagement. We also restricted ourself to the usage of physiological measures to assess "everyday" types of engagement such as reading news and spending time on social networking sites.

Finally, Chapter 4 described measures based on web analytics, which include online behavioral metrics, such as click-through rates, number of page views, time spent on a site (i.e., dwell time), frequency of return visits, etc. This chapter started by differentiating two types of web analytics measures, assessing user engagement within a session and across sessions, respectively. It then discussed other dimensions that have been associated with using web analytics to measure user engagement. The chapter ended with a detailed descriptions of the main types of measures, and gave examples about how to interpret them.

These chapters were followed by two additional chapters. Chapter 5 looked at measuring user engagement in more complex scenarios, acknowledging the ubiquitous computing environment. First, we discussed the concept of multitasking, a behavior that more closely approximates real-world behavior, and then described how web analytics metrics have been adapted to account for it. The chapter then studied this concept in the context of sites offered by large Internet service providers, where the aim is to keep users engaged with their sites, and how to measure this type of engagement. Finally, this chapter looked at user engagement in the context of mobile use, which is important to understand with people spending an increasing amount of time online, not sitting in front of their desktop, but through a mobile device.

The final chapter of this book advocated the adoption of mixed methods, with attention to issues of reliability and validity. The chapter also revisited the basic ideas around scale, temporality, setting, subjectivity/objectivity, and process/product considerations, introduced in Chapter 1.

7.2 FUTURE RESEARCH DIRECTIONS

In much of the work on user engagement, a great deal of emphasis is placed on users—to understand how they engage with a type of application, or on systems—to understand the type of engagement they promote. There was however less emphasis on the role of the task (i.e., what the user is doing), device (desktop versus mobile), and context (e.g., quickly checking something or browsing leisurely). These three dimensions, *task, device, and context*, when considered, are done in a "drill-down" fashion; for example measuring user engagement for a group of users doing a particular task on a particular device in a specific scenario (e.g., when in a hurry). Future work should study user engagement to understand how these dimensions interact in greater depth; how engagement with the same application changes when experienced on a desktop computer compared to on a mobile phone. Research in this direction has already started to appear. For instance, Song et al. [188] and Kamvar et al. [92] showed that desktop users are usually active during working hours, whereas mobile users are more active during the evening; this will have an effect not only on which applications they engage with, but also on how they engage with the same applications.

It will also be important to measure user engagement in situations where users interact with the same application but on a different device, to perform the same task. Take the example of e-shopping. Suppose that a user clicks on an advert while searching on his or her mobile, but then decides to look at the site later on using the desktop. There is a relationship between the two sessions: same intention, same task, but due to some factors, the user decides to postpone interacting with the site until sitting in front of his or her desktop.

Many of the measurement approaches tend to focus on characterizing users in the moment of interaction. But are their individual differences that may predict the level of engagement that can be achieved? It is very likely that a group of users, compared to another one, may be more prone to engage in a particular way with an application. For example, teenagers and older people will interact differently, even on the same application such as the social networking site Facebook. Individual differences may be based on demographics (e.g., gender and age), but it is also likely that there are other variables to consider. It is likely that people who are tech savvy will engage differently with a technology than less tech savvy people. It will also be interesting to understand the relationship between individual different variables and basic engagement attributes to inform design, rather than trying to provide enhanced engagement experience across the board. The research area of personalization should be helpful to develop "personalized-based" measures of engagement.

Psychophysiological measurement may not be sensitive enough to measure "general" or "average" engagement such as those experienced with online news or email sites. Although mouse movements may help us to understand how users engage with search results in the web search scenario, it has proven difficult to generalize to other scenarios. This is not to say that we should not pursue work in this direction. How we "use" physiological measures is an important area for exploration. However, for any measurement that we "think" may be important (e.g., cursor versus interest), we need to made explicit connections to engagement. In particular, it will be important to distinguish between "no signal meaning no indication of engagement or non-engagement" or "no signal meaning wrong or flawed instrumentation." Our research, as described in Chapter 6, clearly shows that this is an important question to address.

Many of the works presented in this book have been carried out on samples drawn entirely from so-called "Western, Educated, Industrialized, Rich, and Democratic" (WEIRD) societies [76]. It has been shown that there are major variations across human populations, and that there is substantial variability in experimental results across populations. Namely, WEIRD subjects are particularly unusual compared with the rest of the species, and are in fact frequent outliers. Thus, it is imperative that the measurement of user engagement should be more inclusive, and go beyond the typical subjects employed in current studies, as any measurements and corresponding outcomes are likely to apply and be valid to very biased populations.

An important future direction is to demonstrate reliability and validity in a more standard fashion, not just in terms of properly employing a methodology when using a particular type of measurement approach. Most papers published in the literature follow methodologies that to some degree encompass some level of validity and reliability verification. However, due to the nature of user engagement, being multifaceted, three main measurements have been carried out. We are in the lucky position that each of them can inform the others, not only in terms of overall better measurements and corresponding understanding, but in terms of reliability and validity of the measures themselves. More work is needed to see how measures from one type of approaches align with that of another one. Some work in that direction has started, as discussed in Chapter 6, but this is just beginning.

7.3   TAKE-AWAYS

To conclude, we articulate the main take-away messages related to how user engagement should be measured.

First no one measure is perfect or complete. Because of the multifaceted nature of user engagement, it is important to look at various ways to measure engagement, ideally across the three types of approaches, self-report, physiological, and web analytics. If this is not possible, or simply not necessary, then it is important to employ several measures of the same type to examine issues of reliability and validity.

The web analytics community has already done this, as dashboards always contain numerous measures. Self-report studies also do the same, as for example questionnaires look at various aspects, such as aesthetics and focused attention. Finally, physiological sensors do record numerous signals, which lead to various measures. Decisions and strategies should never be based on a single measure.

All studies have different constraints. It could be that what the research really needs to know is how users really feel about their engagement with an application, for example, whether the interaction is novel or similar to what has been experienced in the past. In other cases, it is enough to record all user interactions if the aim is to have users spending time on the site. There are also financial, equipment and expertise constraints. Running user studies requires time to design the study, costs for equipment (e.g., eye tracker) and to compensate participants. With respect to equipment, the recording of physiological measures requires expensive and often cumbersome equipment, which may not be an option for some researchers or a one-off study. These types of equipment (e.g., fRMI, eye trackers) are often only available in larger research labs. Finally, there are constraints related to expertise. Implementing mouse tracking is not difficult but needs to be done carefully so as not to affect latency; designing and deploying questionnaires is a task that has to be undertaken carefully; interpreting web analytics as well as developing new metrics requires a strong data science background.

We need to ensure that methods are applied consistently with attention to reliability and validity. Method bias highlights the need for well-constructed measures that have been tested for reliability and validity. At a basic level, reliable measures and methods produce consistent findings in similar circumstances. Validity pertains to how accurately the measure or method captures the phenomenon of interest. Internal validity is focused on what occurs during the study, whereas external validity is concerned with how well the results generalize to the real world.

Finally, more emphasis should be placed on using mixed methods to improve the validity of the measures. It will allow us to derive a better understanding of how to measure user engagement and interpret measurement outcomes, but more importantly, with sufficient time and attention, ensure the reliability and validity of various measures. If we consider the value of user engagement to academic and industry researchers and to users themselves, then surely a more rigorous approach to measurement is warranted.

Bibliography

[1] O.O. Aalen, O. Borgan, and H.K. Gjessing. *Survival and Event History Analysis: A Process Point of View*. Statistics for Biology and Health. Springer, 2008. DOI: 10.1007/978-0-387-68560-1. 78

[2] Rafa Absar, Heather O'Brien, and Helen Halbert. Toward a model of mobile user engagement. In *7th Annual Symposium on Human-Computer Interaction and Information Retrieval (HCIR 2013)*, 2013. 71

[3] Atul Adya, Paramvir Bahl, and Lili Qiu. Analyzing the browse patterns of mobile clients. In *SIGCOMM Workshop on Internet Measurement*, 2001. DOI: 10.1145/505202.505226. 69

[4] Ritu Agarwal and Elena Karahanna. Time flies when you're having fun: Cognitive absorption and beliefs about information technology usage. *MIS Quarterly*, 24(4):665–694, 2000. DOI: 10.2307/3250951. 84

[5] Eugene Agichtein, Eric Brill, and Susan Dumais. Improving web search ranking by incorporating user behavior information. In *Proceedings of the 29th annual international ACM SIGIR conference on Research and development in information retrieval*, SIGIR '06, pages 19–26. ACM, 2006. DOI: 10.1145/1148170.1148177. 39, 41, 81

[6] Eugene Agichtein, Ryen W. White, Susan T. Dumais, and Paul N. Bennet. Search, interrupted: Understanding and predicting search task continuation. In *Proceedings of the 35th International ACM SIGIR Conference on Research and Development in Information Retrieval*, SIGIR '12, pages 315–324, 2012. DOI: 10.1145/2348283.2348328. 64

[7] S. Ahuja, Jaspreet and Jane Webster. Perceived disorientation: An examination of a new measure to assess web design effectiveness. *Interacting with Computers*, 14:15–29, 2001. DOI: 10.1016/S0953-5438(01)00048-0. 28

[8] Jennifer Allanson and Stephen H. Fairclough. A research agenda for physiological computing. *Interacting with Computers*, 16(5):857–878, 2004. DOI: 10.1016/j.intcom.2004.08.001. 31

[9] I. Arapakis, B. Cambazoglu, and M. Lalmas. Understanding within-content engagement through pattern analysis of mouse gestures. In *Proceedings of the 23rd ACM international conference on Information and knowledge management*, CIKM '14. ACM, 2014. xv, 76, 82, 84

[10] Ioannis Arapakis, Konstantinos Athanasakos, and Joemon M. Jose. A comparison of general vs personalised affective models for the prediction of topical relevance. In *Proceedings of the 33rd International ACM SIGIR Conference on Research and Development in Information Retrieval*, SIGIR '10, pages 371–378. ACM, 2010. DOI: 10.1145/1835449.1835512. 34

[11] Ioannis Arapakis, Mounia Lalmas, B. Barla Cambazoglu, Mari-Carmen Marcos, and Joemon M. Jose. User engagement in online news: Under the scope of sentiment, interest, affect, and gaze. *Journal of the Association for Information Science and Technology*, 2014. DOI: 10.1002/asi.23096. xv, 35, 36, 37, 75, 82

[12] Ioannis Arapakis, Mounia Lalmas, Hakan Ceylan, and Pinar Donmez. Automatically embedding newsworthy links to articles: From implementation to evaluation. *JASIST*, 65(1):129–145, 2014. DOI: 10.1002/asi.22959. 77

[13] Ritu Argawal and Elena Karahanna. Time flies when you're having fun: Cognitive absorption beliefs about information technology use. *MIS Quarterly*, 24(4):665–694, 2000. DOI: 10.2307/3250951. 29

[14] MaryAnne Atkinson and Christine T. Kydd. Individual characteristics associated with world wide web use: An empirical study of playfulness and motivation. *DATA BASE*, 28(2):53–62, 1997. DOI: 10.1145/264701.264705. 28

[15] Simon Attfield, Gabriella Kazai, Mounia Lalmas, and Benjamin Piwowarski. Towards a science of user engagement (Position Paper). In *WSDM Workshop on User Modelling for Web Applications*, WSDM '11, Hong Kong, China, 2011. ACM. xv, 2, 3, 4, 87

[16] Daniel Baldauf, Esther Burgard, and Marc Wittmann. Time perception as a workload measure in simulated car driving. *Applied Ergonomics*, 40(5):929 – 935, 2009. DOI: 10.1016/j.apergo.2009.01.004. 4

[17] Roja Bandari, Sitaram Asur, and Bernardo A. Huberman. The pulse of news in social media: Forecasting popularity. In *Proceedings of the Sixth International Conference on Weblogs and Social Media, Dublin, Ireland, June 4-7, 2012*, 2012. 8

[18] Firdaus Banhawi and Nazlena Mohamed Ali. Measuring user engagement attributes in social networking applications. In *Proceedings of the 2011 International Conference on Semantic Technology and Information Retrieval*, pages 297–301, 2011. DOI: 10.1109/STAIR.2011.5995805. 25, 26

[19] Liam J. Bannon. A human-centred perspective on interaction design. In Antti Pirhonen, Pertti Saariluoma, Hannakaisa Isomäki, and Chris Roast, editors, *Future Interaction Design*, pages 31–51. Springer London, 2005. DOI: 10.1007/b138650. 2

[20] Katja Battarbee and Ilpo Koskinen. Co-experience: user experience as interaction. *CoDesign*, 1(1):5–18, 2005. DOI: 10.1080/15710880412331289917. 69

[21] Hila Becker, Andrei Z. Broder, Evgeniy Gabrilovich, Vanja Josifovski, and Bo Pang. What happens after an ad click?: quantifying the impact of landing pages in web advertising. In *Proceedings of the 18th ACM Conference on Information and Knowledge Management, CIKM 2009, Hong Kong, China, November 2-6, 2009*, pages 57–66, 2009. DOI: 10.1145/1645953.1645964. 52

[22] Fabrício Benevenuto, Tiago Rodrigues, Meeyoung Cha, and Virgílio Almeida. Characterizing user behavior in online social networks. In *Proceedings of the 9th ACM SIGCOMM conference on Internet measurement conference*, pages 49–62. ACM, 2009. DOI: 10.1145/1644893.1644900. 50, 53

[23] Bruce L. Berg. *Qualitative Research Methods for the Social Sciences*. Allyn and Bacon, 7 edition, 2008. 16

[24] Mikhail Bilenko and Ryen W. White. Mining the search trails of surfing crowds: identifying relevant websites from user activity. In *17th international conference on World Wide Web*, pages 51–60, 2008. DOI: 10.1145/1367497.1367505. 81

[25] Susanne Bodker. Second wave hci meets third wave challenges. In *NordCHI '06 Extended Abstracts on Human Factors in Computing Systems*, NrodiCHI '06, pages 1–8. ACM, 2006. DOI: 10.1145/1182475.1182476. 1

[26] Jennifer L Branch. Investigating the information-seeking processes of adolescents: The value of using think alouds and think afters. *Library & Information Science Research*, 22(4):371–392, 2000. DOI: 10.1016/S0740-8188(00)00051-7. 19

[27] Joanna Brenner. Pew internet: Mobile., December 2012. 68

[28] John Brooke. Sus-a quick and dirty usability scale. *Usability evaluation in industry*, 189:194, 1996. 84

[29] Andrew Burton-Jones. Minimizing method bias through programmatic research. *MIS Quarterly*, 33(3):445–471, 2009. 13

[30] Georg Buscher, Ralf Biedert, Daniel Heinesch, and Andreas Dengel. Eye tracking analysis of preferred reading regions on the screen. In *Proceedings of the 28th of the International Conference extended abstracts on Human Factors in Computing S*, CHI EA '10, pages 3307–3312, 2010. DOI: 10.1145/1753846.1753976. 36

[31] Georg Buscher, Andreas Dengel, and Ludger van Elst. Query expansion using gaze-based feedback on the subdocument level. In *Proceedings of the 31st annual international ACM*

SIGIR conference on Research and development in information retrieval, SIGIR '08, pages 387–394, 2008. DOI: 10.1145/1390334.1390401. 36

[32] Georg Buscher, Susan T. Dumais, and Edward Cutrell. The good, the bad, and the random: An eye-tracking study of ad quality in web search. In *Proceedings of the 33rd International ACM SIGIR Conference on Research and Development in Information Retrieval*, SIGIR '10, pages 42–49, 2010. DOI: 10.1145/1835449.1835459. 36

[33] Georg Buscher, Ryen W. White, Susan Dumais, and Jeff Huang. Large-scale analysis of individual and task differences in search result page examination strategies. In *Proceedings of the fifth ACM international conference on Web search and data mining*, WSDM '12, pages 373–382, 2012. DOI: 10.1145/2124295.2124341. 41

[34] Lara D. Catledge and James E. Pitkow. Characterizing browsing strategies in the world-wide web. In *Proceedings of the Third International World-Wide Web Conference on Technology, Tools and Applications*, pages 1065–1073, 1995. DOI: 10.1016/0169-7552(95)00043-7. 52

[35] Peter Chapman, Sanjeebhan Selvarajah, and Jane Webster. Engagement in mulitmedia training systems. In *Proceedings of the 32nd Hawaii Conference on Systems Science*, pages 1–9. IEEE, 1997. DOI: 10.1109/HICSS.1999.772808. 23

[36] Chao Chen and Sumi Helal. System-wide support for safety in pervasive spaces. *Journal of Ambient Intelligence and Humanized Computing*, 3(2):113–123, November 2011. DOI: 10.1007/s12652-011-0078-7. 24

[37] Mon Chu Chen, John R. Anderson, and Myeong Ho Sohn. What can a mouse cursor tell us more?: correlation of eye/mouse movements on web browsing. In *CHI '01 extended abstracts on Human factors in computing systems*, CHI '01, pages 281–282, Seattle, Washington, 2001. ACM Press. DOI: 10.1145/634067.634234. 38, 39, 41, 56

[38] Monchu Chen and Veraneka Lim. Eye gaze and mouse cursor relationship in a debugging task. In Constantine Stephanidis, editor, *HCI International 2013 - Posters' Extended Abstracts*, volume 373 of *Communications in Computer and Information Science*, pages 468–472. Springer Berlin Heidelberg, 2013. DOI: 10.1007/978-3-642-39473-7. 39, 76

[39] Karen Church and Nuria Oliver. Understanding mobile web and mobile search use in today's dynamic mobile landscape. In *Proceedings of the 13th International Conference on Human Computer Interaction with Mobile Devices and Services*, pages 67–76. ACM, 2011. DOI: 10.1145/2037373.2037385. 69

[40] Karen Church and Barry Smyth. Understanding the intent behind mobile information needs. In *Proceedings of the 14th international conference on Intelligent user interfaces*, pages 247–256. ACM, 2009. DOI: 10.1145/1502650.1502686. 69

[41] Elizabeth Churchill. Enticing engagement. *interactions*, 17(3):82–87, 2010. DOI: 10.1145/1744161.1744180. 8

[42] Mark Claypool, Phong Le, Makoto Wased, and David Brown. Implicit interest indicators. In *Proceedings of the 6th international conference on Intelligent user interfaces*, IUI '01, pages 33–40. ACM, 2001. DOI: 10.1145/359784.359836. 42, 43

[43] Scott Counts and Kristie Fisher. Taking it all in? visual attention in microblog consumption. In *Proceedings of the Fifth International Conference on Weblogs and Social Media*, ICWSM '11. The AAAI Press, July 2011. 36

[44] Mihaly Csikszentmihalyi. *Flow: The Psychology of Optimal Experience*. Harper and Row, 1990. 4, 29

[45] Edward Cutrell and Zhiwei Guan. What are you looking for?: an eye-tracking study of information usage in web search. In *Proceedings of the SIGCHI Conference on Human Factors in Computing Systems*, CHI '07, pages 407–416, 2007. DOI: 10.1145/1240624.1240690. 38

[46] Fernando Diaz, Ryen W. White, Dan Liebling, and Georg Buscher. Robust models of mouse movement on dynamic web search results pages. In *Proceedings of the 22nd ACM International Conference on Information and Knowledge Management*, CIKM '13. ACM, 2013. DOI: 10.1145/2505515.2505717. 42

[47] Florin Dobrian, Vyas Sekar, Asad Awan, Ion Stoica, Dilip Antony Joseph, Aditya Ganjam, Jibin Zhan, and Hui Zhang. Understanding the impact of video quality on user engagement. *SIGCOMM-Computer Communication Review*, 41(4):362, 2011. DOI: 10.1145/2043164.2018478. 53, 57

[48] Georges Dupret and Mounia Lalmas. Absence time and user engagement: evaluating ranking functions. In *Proceedings of the sixth ACM international conference on Web search and data mining*, pages 173–182. ACM, 2013. DOI: 10.1145/2433396.2433418. xv, 58, 78, 79

[49] Andy Edmonds, Ryen W. White, Dan Morris, and Steven M. Drucker. Instrumenting the dynamic web. *Journal of Web*, 6(3):244–260, 2007. 38, 41

[50] Carsten Eickhoff, Christopher G. Harris, Arjen P. de Vries, and Padmini Srinivasan. Quality through flow and immersion: gamifying crowdsourced relevance assessments. In *The 35th International ACM SIGIR conference on research and development in Information Retrieval*, SIGIR '12, Portland, OR, USA, August 12-16, 2012, pages 871–880, 2012. DOI: 10.1145/2348283.2348400. 77

[51] Nicole B. Ellison, Charles Steinfeld, and Cliff Lampe. The benefits of facebook "friends:" Social capital and college students' use of online social network sites. *Journal of Computer-Mediated Communication*, 12:1143–1168, 2007. DOI: 10.1111/j.1083-6101.2007.00367.x. 57

[52] K. Anders Ericsson. Protocol analysis and expert thought: Concurrent verbalizations of thinking during experts' performance on representative tasks. In *The Cambridge handbook of expertise and expert performance*, pages 223–241. Cambridge University Press New York, 2006. DOI: 10.1017/CBO9780511816796.013. 19

[53] K Anders Ericsson and Herbert A Simon. Verbal reports as data. *Psychological review*, 87(3):215, 1980. DOI: 10.1037/0033-295X.87.3.215. 18

[54] K. Anders Ericsson and Herbert A. Simon. *Protocol analysis: Verbal reports as data*. Cambridge, MA: MIT Press, 1984. 18

[55] Stephen H. Fairclough. Fundamentals of physiological computing. *Interacting with Computers*, 21(1-2):133–145, 2009. DOI: 10.1016/j.intcom.2008.10.011. 32

[56] Martin H. Fischer. An investigation of attention allocation during sequential eye movement tasks. *The Quarterly Journal of Experimental Psychology Section A: Human Experimental Psychology*, 52(3):649–677, 1999. DOI: 10.1080/027249899391007. 36

[57] John C. Flanagan. The critical incident technique. *Psychological Bulletin*, 51(4):327–358, 1954. DOI: 10.1037/h0061470. 17

[58] Andrea Fontant and James H. Frey. The interview: From neutral stance to political involvement. In *The Sage Handbook of Qualitative Research*, pages 695–727. Sage, 2005. 15, 16

[59] Mark C Fox, K Anders Ericsson, and Ryan Best. Do procedures for verbal reporting of thinking have to be reactive? a meta-analysis and recommendations for best reporting methods. *Psychological bulletin*, 137(2):316, 2011. DOI: 10.1037/a0021663. 19

[60] Steve Fox, Kuldeep Karnawat, Mark Mydland, Susan Dumais, and Thomas White. Evaluating implicit measures to improve web search. *ACM Transactions on Information Systems*, 23(2):147–168, April 2005. DOI: 10.1145/1059981.1059982. 42

[61] Jonathan Freeman, Rick Dale, and Thomas Farmer. Hand in motion reveals mind in motion. *Frontiers in Psychology*, 2(59), 2011. DOI: 10.3389/fpsyg.2011.00059. 44

[62] Sara M. Fulmer and Jan C. Frijters. A review of self-report and alternative approaches in the measurement of student motivation. *Educational Psychology Review*, 21(3):219–246, 2009. DOI: 10.1007/s10648-009-9107-x. 11, 12

[63] Jeremy Goecks and Jude Shavlik. Learning users' interests by unobtrusively observing their normal behavior. In *Proceedings of the 5th international conference on Intelligent user interfaces*, IUI '00, pages 129–132, 2000. DOI: 10.1145/325737.325806. 43

[64] Ayşe Göker and Hans Myrhaug. Evaluation of a mobile information system in context. *Information processing & management*, 44(1):39–65, 2008. DOI: 10.1016/j.ipm.2007.03.011. 69

[65] Jennifer Golbeck. Weaving a web of trust. *Science*, 321(5896):1640–1641, 2008. DOI: 10.1126/science.1163357. 6

[66] Qi Guo and Eugene Agichtein. Exploring mouse movements for inferring query intent. In *Proceedings of the 31st annual international ACM SIGIR conference on Research and development in information retrieval*, SIGIR '08, pages 707–708, 2008. DOI: 10.1145/1390334.1390462. 42

[67] Qi Guo and Eugene Agichtein. Ready to buy or just browsing?: detecting web searcher goals from interaction data. In *Proceedings of the 33rd international ACM SIGIR conference on Research and development in information retrieval*, SIGIR '10, pages 130–137. ACM, 2010. DOI: 10.1145/1835449.1835473. 38

[68] Qi Guo and Eugene Agichtein. Towards predicting web searcher gaze position from mouse movements. In *CHI '10 Extended Abstracts on Human Factors in Computing Systems*, CHI EA '10, pages 3601–3606. ACM, 2010. DOI: 10.1145/1753846.1754025. 38, 40

[69] Qi Guo and Eugene Agichtein. Beyond dwell time: estimating document relevance from cursor movements and other post-click searcher behavior. In *Proceedings of the 21st international conference on World Wide Web*, WWW '12, pages 569–578. ACM, 2012. DOI: 10.1145/2187836.2187914. 38, 43

[70] Qi Guo, Dmitry Lagun, and Eugene Agichtein. Predicting web search success with fine-grained interaction data. In *Proceedings of the 21st ACM international conference on Information and knowledge management*, CIKM '12, pages 2050–2054, 2012. DOI: 10.1145/2396761.23985704. 41

[71] Jacek Gwizdka. Characterizing relevance with eye-tracking measures. In *Proceedings of the 5th Information Interaction in Context Symposium*, IIiX '14, pages 58–67, 2014. DOI: 10.1145/2637002.2637011. 75, 85

[72] Martyn Hammersley. Objectivity. pages 751–752. Sage, 2004. 8

[73] Sandra G. Hart and Lowell E. Staveland. Development of NASA-TLX (Task Load Index): Results of Empirical and Theoretical Research. *Human Mental Workload*, 52:139–183, 1988. DOI: 10.1016/S0166-4115(08)62386-9. 27

[74] Marc Hassenzahl and Noam Tractinsky. User experience: a research agenda. *Behaviour and Information Technology*, 25(2):91–97, 2006. DOI: 10.1080/01449290500330331. 1, 3

[75] John M. Henderson. Human gaze control during real-world scene perception. *Trends in Cognitive Sciences*, 7(11):498–504, November 2003. DOI: 10.1016/j.tics.2003.09.006. 36

[76] Joseph Henrich, Steven J. Heine, and Ara Norenzayan. The weirdest people in the world? *Behavioral and Brain Sciences*, 33:61–83, 6 2010. DOI: 10.1017/S0140525X0999152X. 89

[77] Eelco Herder. Characterizations of user web revisit behavior. In *Lernen, Wissensentdeckung und Adaptivität (LWA) 2005, GI Workshops, Saarbrücken, October 10th-12th, 2005*, pages 32–37, 2005. 62

[78] G. Hotchkiss, S. Alston, and G. Edwards. Eye tracking study, 2005. 37

[79] Jeff Huang, Ryen White, and Georg Buscher. User see, user point: Gaze and cursor alignment in web search. In *Proceedings of the SIGCHI Conference on Human Factors in Computing Systems*, CHI '12, pages 1341–1350, 2012. DOI: 10.1145/2207676.2208591. 38, 40, 41

[80] Jeff Huang and Ryen W. White. Parallel browsing behavior on the web. In *Proceedings of the 21st ACM Conference on Hypertext and Hypermedia*, HT '10, pages 13–18, 2010. DOI: 10.1145/1810617.1810622. 53

[81] Jeff Huang, Ryen W. White, and Susan Dumais. No clicks, no problem: using cursor movements to understand and improve search. In *Proceedings of the SIGCHI Conference on Human Factors in Computing Systems*, CHI '11, pages 1225–1234, 2011. DOI: 10.1145/1978942.1979125. 38, 39, 40, 41, 56

[82] Edwin L. Hutchins, James D. Hollan, and Donald A. Norman. Direct manipulation interfaces. *Hum.-Comput. Interact.*, 1(4):311–338, December 1985. DOI: 10.1207/s15327051hci0104_2. 2

[83] José Antonio Hyder Espineira. *Proposal of a website engagement scale and research model. Analysis of the influence of intra-website comparative behavior.* University of Valencia (Spain), 2010. 25, 26

[84] W.A. Ijsselstein, H. de Ridder, and J. Freemanand S.E. Avons. Presence: Concept, determinants and measurement. In *SPIE*, 2000. DOI: 10.1117/12.387188. 9, 81

[85] Matthew O Jackson. *Social and economic networks*. Princeton University Press, 2010. 57

[86] S. Jackson. *Cult of Analytics: Driving online marketing strategies using web analytics*. Taylor & Francis, 2012. 55

[87] R. D. Jacques. *The Nature of Engagement and its Role in Hypermedia Evaluation and Design.* Phd thesis, South Bank University, London, 1996. 2, 3, 4, 16, 17, 18, 22, 23

[88] Bernard J. Jansen and Michael D. McNeese. Evaluating the effectiveness of and patterns of interactions with automated searching assistance. *Journal of the American Society for Information Science and Technology*, 56(14):1480–1503, 2005. DOI: 10.1002/asi.20242. 81

[89] Charlene Jennett, Anna L. Cox, Paul Cairns, Samira Dhoparee, Andrew Epps, Tim Tijs, and Alison Walton. Measuring and defining the experience of immersion in games. *International Journal of Human-Computer Studies*, 66(9):641–661, September 2008. DOI: 10.1016/j.ijhcs.2008.04.004. 4, 10, 31

[90] Morgan Jennings. Theory and models for creating engaging and immersive ecommerce websites. In *SIGCPR*, pages 77–85, 2000. DOI: 10.1145/333334.333358. 4, 5

[91] Reynol Junco. Comparing actual and self-reported measures of facebook use. *Computers in Human Behavior*, 29:626–631, 2013. DOI: 10.1016/j.chb.2012.11.007. 13

[92] Maryam Kamvar and Shumeet Baluja. A large scale study of wireless search behavior: Google mobile search. In *Proceedings of the 2006 Conference on Human Factors in Computing Systems, CHI 2006, Montréal, Québec, Canada, April 22-27, 2006*, pages 701–709, 2006. DOI: 10.1145/1124772.1124877. 68, 89

[93] Evangelos Karapanos, Jhilmil Jain, and Marc Hassenzahl. Theories, methods and case studies of longitudinal hci research. In *CHI '12 Extended Abstracts on Human Factors in Computing Systems*, CHI EA '12, pages 2727–2730, 2012. DOI: 10.1145/2212776.2212706. 80

[94] Gabriella Kazai and Natasa Milic-Frayling. Effects of social approval votes on search performance. In *Sixth International Conference on Information Technology: New Generations, ITNG 2009, Las Vegas, Nevada, 27-29 April 2009*, pages 1554–1559, 2009. DOI: 10.1109/ITNG.2009.281. 6

[95] Melanie Kellar, Carolyn Watters, and Michael Shepherd. A field study characterizing web-based information-seeking tasks. *Journal of the American Society for Information Science and Technology*, 58(7):999–1018, 2007. DOI: 10.1002/asi.20590. 35, 77

[96] Diane Kelly. Methods for evaluating interactive information retrieval systems with users. *Foundations and Trends in Information Retrieval*, 3:1–224, 2009. DOI: 10.1561/1500000012. 13, 14, 15, 18, 19, 22, 26

[97] Diane Kelly and Nicholas J. Belkin. Reading time, scrolling and interaction: exploring implicit sources of user preferences for relevance feedback. In *Proceedings of the 24th annual international ACM SIGIR conference on Research and development in information retrieval*, SIGIR '01, pages 408–409. ACM, 2001. DOI: 10.1145/383952.384045. 42

[98] Diane Kelly and Nicholas J. Belkin. Display time as implicit feedback: understanding task effects. In *Proceedings of the 27th annual international ACM SIGIR conference on Research and development in information retrieval*, SIGIR '04, pages 377–384. ACM, 2004. DOI: 10.1145/1008992.1009057. 42

[99] Diane Kelly, David J Harper, and Brian Landau. Questionnaire mode effects in interactive information retrieval experiments. *Information processing & management*, 44(1):122–141, 2008. DOI: 10.1016/j.ipm.2007.02.007. 20, 21, 82

[100] Rohit Khare and Adam Rifkin. Trust management on the world wide web. *First Monday*, 3(6), 1998. DOI: 10.1016/S0169-7552(98)00091-9. 6

[101] Michael Khoo, Joe Pagano, Anne L. Washington, Mimi Recker, Bart Palmer, and Robert A. Donahue. Using web metrics to analyze digital libraries. In *8th ACM/IEEE-CS joint conference on Digital libraries*, pages 375–384, 2008. DOI: 10.1145/1378889.1378956. 8

[102] Eunice Kim, Jhih-Syuan Lin, and Yongjun Sung. To app or not to app: Engaging consumers via branded mobile apps. *Journal of Interactive Advertising*, 13(1):53–65, 2013. DOI: 10.1080/15252019.2013.782780. 70

[103] Youngho Kim, Ahmed Hassan Awadallah, Ryen W. White, and Imed Zitouni. Modeling dwell time to predict click-level satisfaction. In *Seventh ACM International Conference on Web Search and Data Mining, WSDM 2014, New York, NY, USA, February 24-28, 2014*, pages 193–202, 2014. DOI: 10.1145/2556195.2556220. 52

[104] Tetsuro Kobayashi and Jeffrey Boase. No such effect? the implications of measurement error in self-report measures of mobile communication use. *Communication Methods and Measures*, 6(2):126–143, 2012. DOI: 10.1080/19312458.2012.679243. 13

[105] Ron Kohavi, Alex Deng, Brian Frasca, Roger Longbotham, Toby Walker, and Ya Xu. Trustworthy online controlled experiments: Five puzzling outcomes explained. In *Proceedings of the 18th ACM SIGKDD international conference on Knowledge discovery and data mining*, pages 786–794. ACM, 2012. DOI: 10.1145/2339530.2339653. 47, 55, 58

[106] Daijiro Komaki, Takahiro Hara, and Shojiro Nishio. How does mobile context affect people's web search behavior?: A diary study of mobile information needs and search behaviors. In *Advanced Information Networking and Applications (AINA), 2012 IEEE 26th International Conference on*, pages 245–252. IEEE, 2012. DOI: 10.1109/AINA.2012.134. 69

[107] Emiel Krahmer and Nicole Ummelen. Thinking about thinking aloud: A comparison of two verbal protocols for usability testing. *Professional Communication, IEEE Transactions on*, 47(2):105–117, 2004. DOI: 10.1109/TPC.2004.828205. 19

[108] Ravi Kumar and Andrew Tomkins. A characterization of online browsing behavior. In *Proceedings of the 19th International Conference on World Wide Web*, WWW '10, pages 561–570, 2010. DOI: 10.1145/1772690.1772748. 62

[109] D. Lagun, C.-H. Hsieh, D. Webster, and V. Navalpakkam. Towards better measurement of attention and satisfaction in mobile search. In *Proceedings of ACM SIGIR conference on Research and development in information retrieval*, SIGIR '10. ACM, 2014. DOI: 10.1145/2600428.2609631. 70, 76

[110] Dmitry Lagun, Mikhail Ageev, Qi Guo, and Eugene Agichtein. Discovering common motifs in cursor movement data for improving web search. In *Proceedings of the 7th ACM International Conference on Web Search and Data Mining*, WSDM '14, pages 183–192, 2014. DOI: 10.1145/2556195.2556265. 41

[111] Dmitry Lagun and Eugene Agichtein. Viewser: enabling large-scale remote user studies of web search examination and interaction. In *Proceeding of the 34th International ACM SIGIR Conference on Research and Development in Information Retrieval*, pages 365–374, 2011. DOI: 10.1145/2009916.2009967. 38, 40

[112] M. Lalmas, J. Lehmann, G. Shaked, F. Silvestri, and G. Tolomei. Measuring post-click user experience with mobile native advertising on streams. In *Submitted for Publication*, 2014. 81

[113] P. J. Lang. The emotion probe: Studies of motivation and attention. *American Psychologist*, pages 372–385, 1995. DOI: 10.1037/0003-066X.50.5.372. 33

[114] Reed Larson and Mihaly Csikszentmihalyi. The experience sampling method. *New Directions for Methodology of Social & Behavioral Science*, 15:41–56, 1983. 80

[115] B. Laurel. *Computers as Theatre*. Reading, MA: Addison-Wesley, 1993. 2

[116] Talia Lavie and Noam Tractinsky. Assessing dimensions of perceived visual aesthetics of web sites. *International journal of human-computer studies*, 60(3):269–298, 2004. DOI: 10.1016/j.ijhcs.2003.09.002. 5, 22

[117] Effie Lai-Chong Law, Virpi Roto, Marc Hassenzahl, Arnold P. O. S. Vermeeren, and Joke Kort. Understanding, scoping and defining user experience: a survey approach. In *Proceedings of the 27th International Conference on Human Factors in Computing Systems, CHI 2009, Boston, MA, USA, April 4-9, 2009*, pages 719–728, 2009. DOI: 10.1145/1518701.1518813. 7

[118] Chung Tong Lee, Eduarda Mendes Rodrigues, Gabriella Kazai, Natasa Milic-Frayling, and Aleksandar Ignjatovic. Model for voter scoring and best answer selection in community q&a services. In *Web Intelligence*, pages 116–123, 2009. DOI: 10.1109/WI-IAT.2009.23. 6

[119] R. Craig Lefebvre, Yuri Tada, Sandra W. Hilfiker, and Cynthia Baur. The assessment of user engagement with ehealth content: The ehealth engagement scale. *Journal of Computer-Mediated Communication*, 15:666–681, 2010. DOI: 10.1111/j.1083-6101.2009.01514.x. 22, 26

[120] Janette Lehmann, Mounia Lalmas, Ricardo A. Baeza-Yates, and Elad Yom-Tov. Networked user engagement. In *CIKM workshop on User Engagement Optimization*, 2013. DOI: 10.1145/2512875.2512877. 79, 85

[121] Janette Lehmann, Mounia Lalmas, Georges Dupret, and Ricardo Baeza-Yates. Online multitasking and user engagement. In *Proceedings of the 22Nd ACM International Conference on Conference on Information and Knowledge Management*, CIKM '13, pages 519–528, 2013. DOI: 10.1145/2505515.2505543. xv, 53, 54, 62, 63, 85

[122] Janette Lehmann, Mounia Lalmas, Elad Yom-tov, and Georges Dupret. Models of User Engagement. In *20th conference on User Modeling, Adaptation, and Personalization*, 2012. DOI: 10.1007/978-3-642-31454-4_14. xv, 48, 49, 50, 51

[123] Vincent Levesque, Louise Oram, Karon MacLean, Andy Cockburn, Nicholas Marchuk, Dan Johnson, J. Edward Colgate, and Michael Peshkin. Functional widgets: Enhancing touch interfaces with programmable friction. In *Proceedings of the SIGCHI Conference on Human Factors in Computing*, pages 1153–1158. ACM, 2011. DOI: 10.1145/1979742.1979713. 25, 26

[124] Gitte Lindgaard, Gary Fernandes, Cathy Dudek, and J. Brown. Attention web designers: You have 50 milliseconds to make a good first impression! *Behaviour & Information Technology*, 25(2):115–126, 2006. DOI: 10.1080/01449290500330448. 5

[125] Luca Longo. Human-computer interaction and human mental workload: Assessing cognitive engagement in the world wide web. In *Proceedings of INTERACT 2011, Part IV, LNCS 6949*, pages 402–405. Springer, 2011. DOI: 10.1007/978-3-642-23768-3_43. 27

[126] Irene Lopatovska and Ioannis Arapakis. Theories, methods and current research on emotions in library and information science, information retrieval and human computer interaction. *Information Processing and Management*, 47(4):575–592, 2011. DOI: 10.1016/j.ipm.2010.09.001. 12

[127] Claudio Lucchese, Salvatore Orlando, Raffaele Perego, Fabrizio Silvestri, and Gabriele Tolomei. Identifying task-based sessions in search engine query logs. In *Proceedings of the Fourth ACM International Conference on Web Search and Data Mining*, WSDM '11, pages 277–286, 2011. DOI: 10.1145/1935826.1935875. 62, 64

[128] Lili Luo and Barbara Wildemuth. Semistructured interviews. In Barbara Wildemuth, editor, *Applications of Social Research Methods to Questions in Information and Library Science*, pages 232–241. Libraries Unlimited, 2009. 16

[129] Winter Mason and Siddharth Suri. Conducting behavioral research on Amazon's Mechanical Turk. *Behavior Research Methods*, 44(1):1–23, 2012. DOI: 10.3758/s13428-011-0124-6. 77

[130] Winter A. Mason and Duncan J. Watts. Financial incentives and the "performance of crowds". *SIGKDD Explorations*, 11(2):100–108, 2009. DOI: 10.1145/1809400.1809422. 77

[131] Maurizio Mauri, Pietro Cipresso, Anna Balgera, Marco Villamira, and Giuseppe Riva. Why is facebook so successful? psychophysiological measures describe a core flow state while using facebook. *Cyberpsy., Behavior, and Soc. Networking*, 14(12):723–731, 2011. DOI: 10.1089/cyber.2010.0377. 33

[132] Rob McCarney, James Warner, Steve Iliffe, Robbert van Haselen, Mark Griffin, and Peter Fisher. The hawthorne effect: a randomised, controlled trial. *BMC Medical Research Methodology*, 7(1), 2007. DOI: 10.1186/1471-2288-7-30. 83

[133] John McCarthy and Peter Wright. *Technology As Experience*. The MIT Press, 2004. 2

[134] Lori McCay-Peet, Mounia Lalmas, and Vidhya Navalpakkam. On saliency, affect and focused attention. In *ACM SIGCHI Conference on Human Factors in Computing Systems*, CHI '12, pages 541–550, May 2012. DOI: 10.1145/2207676.2207751. xv, 25, 26, 77, 78, 82

[135] Bruce McKenzie and Andy Cockburn. An emprical analysis of web page revisitation. In *HICSS*, 2001. DOI: 10.1109/HICSS.2001.926533. 62

[136] Vicki McKinney, Kanghyun Yoon, and F. Zahedi. The measurement of web-customer satisfaction: an expectation and disconfirmation approach. *Information systems research*, 13(3):296–315, 2002. DOI: 10.1287/isre.13.3.296.76.

[137] Stefano Mizzaro. Relevance: The whole history. *JASIS*, 48(9):810–832, 1997. DOI: 10.1002/(SICI)1097-4571(199709)48:9%3C810::AID-ASI6%3E3.0.CO;2-U. 34

[138] Masahiro Morita and Yoichi Shinoda. Information filtering based on user behavior analysis and best match text retrieval. In *Proceedings of the 17th annual international ACM SIGIR conference on Research and development in information retrieval*, SIGIR '94, pages 272–281. Springer-Verlag New York, Inc., 1994. DOI: 10.1007/978-1-4471-2099-5_28. 42

[139] Yashar Moshfeghi, LuisaR. Pinto, FrankE. Pollick, and JoemonM. Jose. Understanding relevance: An fmri study. In *Advances in Information Retrieval*, volume 7814 of *Lecture Notes in Computer Science*, pages 14–25. 2013. DOI: 10.1007/978-3-642-36973-5_2. 33

[140] Florian Mueller and Andrea Lockerd. Cheese: tracking mouse movement activity on websites, a tool for user modeling. In *CHI '01 Extended Abstracts on Human Factors in Computing Systems*, CHI EA '01, pages 279–280. ACM, 2001. DOI: 10.1145/634067.634233. 43

[141] Lik Mui, Mojdeh Mohtashemi, and Ari Halberstadt. A computational model of trust and reputation for e-businesses. In *HICSS*, page 188, 2002. 6

[142] Vidhya Navalpakkam and Elizabeth Churchill. Mouse tracking: measuring and predicting users' experience of web-based content. In *Proceedings of the SIGCHI Conference on Human Factors in Computing Systems*, CHI '12, pages 2963–2972, 2012. DOI: 10.1145/2207676.2208705. 39, 44, 76

[143] Vidhya Navalpakkam, LaDawn Jentzsch, Rory Sayres, Sujith Ravi, Amr Ahmed, and Alex J. Smola. Measurement and modeling of eye-mouse behavior in the presence of nonlinear page layouts. In *World Wide Web Conference*, pages 953–964, 2013. 40

[144] Vidhya Navalpakkam, Ravi Kumar, Lihong Li, and D. Sivakumar. Attention and selection in online choice tasks. In *User Modeling, Adaptation, and Personalization*, volume 7379, pages 200–211, 2012. DOI: 10.1007/978-3-642-31454-4_17. 37

[145] Mark EJ Newman. The structure and function of complex networks. *SIAM review*, 45(2):167–256, 2003. DOI: 10.1137/S003614450342480. 79

[146] Stina Nylander, Terés Lundquist, Andreas Brännström, and Bo Karlson. "it's just easier with the phone"–a diary study of internet access from cell phones. In *Pervasive Computing*, pages 354–371. Springer, 2009. DOI: 10.1007/978-3-642-01516-8_24. 69, 70

[147] Hartmut Obendorf, Harald Weinreich, Eelco Herder, and Matthias Mayer. Web page revisitation revisited: Implications of a long-term click-stream study of browser usage. In *CHI*, 2007. DOI: 10.1145/1240624.1240719. 62

[148] Heather L. O'Brien. The influence of hedonic and utilitarian motivation on user engagement: The case of online shopping experiences. *Interacting with Computers*, 22(4):344–352, 2010. DOI: 10.1016/j.intcom.2010.04.001. 25, 26

[149] Heather L O'Brien and Mahria Lebow. Mixed-methods approach to measuring user experience in online news interactions. *Journal of the American Society for Information Science and Technology*, 2013. DOI: 10.1002/asi.22871. 20, 84

[150] Heather L. O'Brien and Elaine G. Toms. What is user engagement? a conceptual framework for defining user engagement with technology. *Journal of the American Society for Information Science and Technology*, 59(6):938–955, 2008. DOI: 10.1002/asi.20801. 2, 3, 4, 5, 6, 24, 27, 28, 81

[151] Heather L. O'Brien and Elaine G. Toms. The development and evaluation of a survey to measure user engagement. *Journal of the American Society for Information Science and Technology*, 61(1):50–69, January 2010. DOI: 10.1002/asi.21229. 4, 5, 6, 7, 22, 24

[152] Heather L. O'Brien and Elaine G. Toms. Measuring engagement in search systems using the user engagement scale (ues). *Information Processing and Management*, 49:1092–1107, 2013. 25, 26

[153] Heather L. O'Brien and G. Toms, Elaine. Measuring interactive information retrieval: The case of the user engagement scale. In *Proceedings of the 2010 Conference of Information Interaction in Context*, pages 335–340. ACM, 2010. DOI: 10.1145/1840784.1840835. 25, 26

[154] Heather Lynn O'Brien. *Defining and Measuring Engagement in User Experiences with Technology*. Doctoral thesis, Dalhousie University, 2008. 2, 4, 17

[155] Marianna Obrist, Virpi Roto, and Kaisa Väänänen-Vainio-Mattila. User experience evaluation: do you know which method to use? In *Proceedings of the 27th International Conference on Human Factors in Computing Systems, CHI 2009, Extended Abstracts Volume, Boston, MA, USA, April 4-9, 2009*, pages 2763–2766, 2009. DOI: 10.1145/1520340.1520401. 7

[156] Erica L Olmsted-Hawala, Elizabeth D Murphy, Sam Hawala, and Kathleen T Ashenfelter. Think-aloud protocols: a comparison of three think-aloud protocols for use in testing data-dissemination web sites for usability. In *Proceedings of the SIGCHI Conference on Human Factors in Computing Systems*, pages 2381–2390. ACM, 2010. DOI: 10.1145/1753326.1753685. 19

[157] Antti Oulasvirta, Tye Rattenbury, Lingyi Ma, and Eeva Raita. Habits make smartphone use more pervasive. *Personal and Ubiquitous Computing*, 16(1):105–114, 2012. DOI: 10.1007/s00779-011-0412-2. 70

[158] Antti Oulasvirta, Sakari Tamminen, Virpi Roto, and Jaana Kuorelahti. Interaction in 4-second bursts: the fragmented nature of attentional resources in mobile hci. In *Proceedings of the SIGCHI conference on Human factors in computing systems*, pages 919–928. ACM, 2005. DOI: 10.1145/1054972.1055101. 69, 70

[159] Kees Overbeeke, Tom Djajadiningrat, Caroline Hummels, Stephan Wensveen, and Joep Prens. Let's make things engaging. In MarkA. Blythe, Kees Overbeeke, AndrewF. Monk, and PeterC. Wright, editors, *Funology*, volume 3, pages 7–17. 2003. 2

[160] Lucas Paletta, Katrin Santner, Gerald Fritz, Heinz Mayer, and Johann Schrammel. 3d attention: Measurement of visual saliency using eye tracking glasses. In *CHI '13 Extended Abstracts on Human Factors in Computing Systems*, CHI EA '13, pages 199–204, 2013. DOI: 10.1145/2468356.2468393. 38

[161] Sebastian Pannasch, Johannes Schulz, and Boris M. Velichkovsky. On the control of visual fixation durations in free viewing of complex images. *Attention, Perception, & Psychophysics*, 73(4):1120–1132, 2011. DOI: 10.3758/s13414-011-0090-1. 36

[162] Randy Pausch, Rich Gold, Tim Skelly, and David Thiel. What hci designers can learn from video game designers. In *Conference on Human Factors in Computing Systems, CHI 1994, Boston, Massachusetts, USA, April 24-28, 1994, Conference Companion*, pages 177–178, 1994. DOI: 10.1145/259963.260220. 28

[163] Eric T. Peterson and Joseph Carrabis. Measuring the Immeasurable: Visitor Engagement, 2008. 6

[164] Robert A Peterson. *Constructing Effective Questionnaires*. Sage, 2000. 14, 20, 21

[165] Robert Plutchik. *Emotion: Theory, research, and experience: Vol. 1. Theories of emotion 1*. New York: Academic, 1980. 45

[166] Ashok Kumar Ponnuswami, Kumaresh Pattabiraman, Qiang Wu, Ran Gilad-Bachrach, and Tapas Kanungo. On composition of a federated web search result page: using online users to provide pairwise preference for heterogeneous verticals. In *Proceedings of the fourth ACM international conference on Web search and data mining*, pages 715–724. ACM, 2011. DOI: 10.1145/1935826.1935922. 55

[167] W Quesenbury. *Content and Complexity: Information Design in Technical Communication*. Lawrence Erlbaum Associates, 2003. 2

[168] Ahmad Rahmati and Lin Zhong. Studying smartphone usage: Lessons from a four-month field study. *IEEE Transactions on Mobile Computing*, 12(7), 2013. DOI: 10.1109/TMC.2012.127. 69

[169] Keith Rayner. Eye movements and visual cognition: Scene perception and reading. In K. Rayner, editor, *Springer series in neuropsychology*, pages 46–65. Springer-Verlag, 1992. 36

[170] Janet Read and Stuart Macfarlane. Endurability, engagement and expectations: Measuring children's fun. In *Interaction Design and Children, Shaker Publishing*, pages 1–23. Shaker Publishing, 2002. 5

[171] Gary B. Reid and Thomas E. Nygren. The subjective mental workload assessment technique: A scaling procedure for measuring mental workload. In Peter A. Hancock and Najmedin Meshkati, editors, *Human Mental Workload*, pages 185–218. Elsevier, 1988. 27

[172] R. W. Remington. Attention and saccadic eye movements. *Journal of Experimental Psychology: Human Perception and Performance*, 6(4):726–744, 1980. DOI: 10.1037/0096-1523.6.4.726. 36

[173] Matthew Richardson, Ewa Dominowska, and Robert Ragno. Predicting clicks: estimating the click-through rate for new ads. In *Proceedings of the 16th international conference on World Wide Web*, pages 521–530. ACM, 2007. DOI: 10.1145/1242572.1242643. 55

[174] LloydP. Rieber. Seriously considering play: Designing interactive learning environments based on the blending of microworlds, simulations, and games. *Educational Technology Research and Development*, 44(2):43–58, 1996. DOI: 10.1007/BF02300540. 28

[175] Kerry Rodden, Xin Fu, Anne Aula, and Ian Spiro. Eye-mouse coordination patterns on web search results pages. In *CHI '08 Extended Abstracts on Human Factors in Computing Systems*, CHI EA '08, pages 2997–3002. ACM, 2008. DOI: 10.1145/1358628.1358797. 38, 39, 40, 41, 56

[176] Kerry Rodden, Hilary Hutchinson, and Xin Fu. Measuring the user experience on a large scale: user-centered metrics for web applications. In *CHI Conference on Human Factors in Computing Systems*, pages 2395–2398, 2010. DOI: 10.1145/1753326.1753687. 81

[177] Marco M. C. Rozendaal, David V. Keyson, and Huib de Ridder. Product features and task effects on experienced richness, control and engagement in voicemail browsing. *Personal and Ubiquitous Computing*, 13(5):343–354, 2009. DOI: 10.1007/s00779-008-0201-8. 6

[178] Susana Rubio, Eva Diaz, Jesús Martin, and José M. Puente. Evaluation of subjective mental workload: A comparison of swat, nasa-tlx, and workload profile methods. *Applied Psychology: An International Review*, 53(1):61–86, 2004. DOI: 10.1111/j.1464-0597.2004.00161.x. 27

[179] James A. Russell, Anna Weiss, and Gerald A. Mendelsohn. Affect grid: A single-item scale of pleasure and arousal. *Journal Personality and Social Psychology*, 57(3):493–502, 1988. DOI: 10.1037/0022-3514.57.3.493. 12

[180] F. Saal, R. Downey, and M. Lahey. Rating the ratings: assessing the psychometric quality of rating data. *Psychological Bulletin*, 8(2), 1980. 81

[181] Norma S. Said. An engaging multimedia design model. In *Proceedings of the 2004 Conference on Interaction Design and Children: Building a Community*, IDC '04, pages 169–172. ACM, 2004. DOI: 10.1145/1017833.1017873. 6, 28

[182] J. Saipe. User Experience (UX) and Improving Engagement. E-insight Blog: Usability & UX, 2009. 7

[183] D. Sculley, Robert G. Malkin, Sugato Basu, and Roberto J. Bayardo. Predicting bounce rates in sponsored search advertisements. In *Proceedings of the 15th ACM SIGKDD International Conference on Knowledge Discovery and Data Mining*, KDD '09, pages 1325–1334, 2009. DOI: 10.1145/1557019.1557161. 53

[184] Bracha Shapira, Meirav Taieb-Maimon, and Anny Moskowitz. Study of the usefulness of known and new implicit indicators and their optimal combination for accurate inference of users interests. In *Proceedings of the 2006 ACM symposium on Applied computing*, SAC '06, pages 1118–1119, 2006. DOI: 10.1145/1141277.1141542. 43

[185] M. Shepherd, J. M. Findlay, and R. J. Hockey. The relationship between eye movements and spatial attention. *Quarterly Journal of Experimental Psychology*, 38(3):475–491, August 1986. DOI: 10.1080/14640748608401609. 36

[186] Mark D. Smucker, Xiaoyu Sunny Guo, and Andrew Toulis. Mouse movement during relevance judging: implications for determining user attention. In *The 37th International ACM SIGIR Conference on Research and Development in Information Retrieval, SIGIR '14, Gold Coast , QLD, Australia - July 06 - 11, 2014*, pages 979–982, 2014. DOI: 10.1145/2600428.2609489. 44

[187] Joo-Hyun Song and Ken Nakayama. Hidden cognitive states revealed in choice reaching tasks. *Trends in cognitive sciences*, 13(8):360 – 366, 2009. DOI: 10.1016/j.tics.2009.04.009. 44

[188] Yang Song, Hao Ma, Hongning Wang, and Kuansan Wang. Exploring and exploiting user search behavior on mobile and tablet devices to improve search relevance. In *22nd International World Wide Web Conference, WWW '13, Rio de Janeiro, Brazil, May 13-17, 2013*, pages 1201–1212, 2013. 68, 69, 89

[189] Amanda Spink, Minsoo Park, Bernard J. Jansen, and Jan O. Pedersen. Multitasking during web search sessions. *Inf. Process. Manage.*, 42(1):264–275, 2006. DOI: 10.1016/j.ipm.2004.10.004. 62

[190] W Stephenson. *Play theory*, pages 45–65. 1967. 28

[191] Alistair Sutcliffe. Designing for user engagement: Aesthetic and attractive user interfaces. *Synthesis Lectures on Human-Centered Informatics*, 2(1):1–55, 2009. DOI: 10.2200/S00210ED1V01Y200910HCI005. 2, 10

[192] Ben Swift, Henry Gardner, and Alistair Riddell. Engagement networs in social music-making. In *Proceedings of the 22nd ACM Conference of the Computer-Human Interaction Special Interest Group of Austrailia (OZCHI)*, pages 104–111. ACM, 2010. DOI: 10.1145/1952222.1952244. 16

[193] Jaime Teevan, Amy Karlson, Shahriyar Amini, AJ Brush, and John Krumm. Understanding the importance of location, time, and people in mobile local search behavior. In *Proceedings of the 13th International Conference on Human Computer Interaction with Mobile Devices and Services*, pages 77–80. ACM, 2011. DOI: 10.1145/2037373.2037386. 69

[194] M. Thelwall, K. Buckley, and G. Paltoglou. Sentiment strength detection for the social web. *J. Am. Soc. Inf. Sci. Technol.*, 63(1):163–173, 2012. DOI: 10.1002/asi.21662. 76

[195] Mike Thelwall, Kevan Buckley, and Georgios Paltoglou. Sentiment strength detection for the social web. *JASIST*, 63(1):163–173, 2012. DOI: 10.1002/asi.21662. 37

[196] Dewi Tojib and Yelena Tsarenko. Post-adoption modeling of advanced mobile service use. *Journal of Business Research*, 65(7):922–928, 2012. DOI: 10.1016/j.jbusres.2011.05.006. 69

[197] Elaine G. Toms. Understanding and facilitating the browsing of electronic text. *Int. J. Hum.-Comput. Stud.*, 52(3):423–452, 2000. DOI: 10.1006/ijhc.1999.0345. 28

[198] Noam Tractinsky, A. S. Katz, and D. Ikar. What is beautiful is usable. *Interacting with Computers*, 13(2):127–145, 2000. DOI: 10.1016/S0953-5438(00)00031-X. 5

[199] Pamela S. Tsang and Velma L. Velazquez. Diagnosticity and mulitdimensional subjective workload ratings. *Ergonomics*, 39(3):358–381, 1996. DOI: 10.1080/00140139608964470. 27

[200] Maaike Van Den Haak, Menno De Jong, and Peter Jan Schellens. Retrospective vs. concurrent think-aloud protocols: testing the usability of an online library catalogue. *Behaviour & Information Technology*, 22(5):339–351, 2003. DOI: 10.1080/0044929031000. 19

[201] Robin L Wakefield and Dwayne Whitten. Mobile computing: a user study on hedonic/utilitarian mobile device usage. *European Journal of Information Systems*, 15(3):292–300, 2006. DOI: 10.1057/palgrave.ejis.3000619. 70

[202] Qing Wang and Huiyou Chang. Multitasking bar: prototype and evaluation of introducing the task concept into a browser. In *Proceedings of the 28th International Conference on Human Factors in Computing Systems, CHI 2010, Atlanta, Georgia, USA, April 10-15, 2010*, pages 103–112, 2010. 62

[203] David Warnock and Mounia Lalmas. An Exploration of Cursor Tracking Data. Technical report, Yahoo Labs, 2013. xv, 45, 82, 83

[204] D. Watson, L.A. Clark, and A. Tellegen. Development and validation of brief measures of positive and negative affect: The panas scales. *Journal of Personality and Social Psychology*, 54(6):1063–1070, 1988. DOI: 10.1037/0022-3514.54.6.1063. 12, 25

[205] Jane Webster and S. Ahuja, Jaspreet. Enhancing the design of web navigation systems: The influence of user disorientation on engagement and performance. *MIS Quarterly*, 30(3):661–678, 2006. 23, 24, 27, 28

[206] Jane Webster and Hayes Ho. Audience engagement with multimedia presentations. *The DATABASE for Advances in Information Systems*, 28(2):63–77, 1997. DOI: 10.1145/264701.264706. 2, 4, 6, 18, 22, 23, 24, 27, 29

[207] Jane Webster and Joseph J. Martocchio. Microcomputer playfulness: Development of a measure with workplace implications. *MIS Quarterly*, 14(2):201–226, 1992. DOI: 10.2307/249576. 28

[208] Ryen W. White and Diane Kelly. A study on the effects of personalization and task information on implicit feedback performance. In *Proceedings of the 15th ACM international conference on Information and knowledge management*, CIKM '06, pages 297–306. ACM, 2006. DOI: 10.1145/1183614.1183659. 42

[209] Amy B. Woszczynski, Philip L. Roth, and Albert H. Segars. Exploring the theoretical foundations of playfulness in computer interactions. *Computers in Human Behavior*, 18(4):369–388, 2002. DOI: 10.1016/S0747-5632(01)00058-9. 28

[210] Xing Yi, Liangjie Hong, Erheng Zhong, Nanthan Nan Liu, and Suju Rajan. Beyond clicks: dwell time for personalization. In *Eighth ACM Conference on Recommender Systems, RecSys '14, Foster City, Silicon Valley, CA, USA - October 06 - 10, 2014*, pages 113–120, 2014. DOI: 10.1145/2645710.2645724. 52, 81

[211] Elad Yom-Tov, Mounia Lalmas, Ricardo A. Baeza-Yates, Georges Dupret, Janette Lehmann, and Pinar Donmez. Measuring inter-site engagement. In *Proceedings of the 2013 IEEE International Conference on Big Data, 6-9 October 2013, Santa Clara, CA, USA*, pages 228–236, 2013. DOI: 10.1109/BigData.2013.6691579. xv, 48, 50, 52, 65, 66

[212] Elad Yom-Tov, Mounia Lalmas, Georges Dupret, Ricardo A. Baeza-Yates, Pinar Donmez, and Janette Lehmann. The effect of links on networked user engagement. In *Proceedings of the 21st World Wide Web Conference, WWW 2012, Lyon, France, April 16-20, 2012 (Companion Volume)*, pages 641–642, 2012. DOI: 10.1145/2187980.2188167. xv, 67

Authors' Biographies

MOUNIA LALMAS

Mounia Lalmas is a Principal Research Scientist at Yahoo Labs London. Prior to this, she held a Microsoft Research/RAEng Research Chair at University of Glasgow. Before that, she was Professor of Information Retrieval at Queen Mary, University of London. From 2002 until 2007, she co-led the Evaluation Initiative for XML Retrieval (INEX), a large-scale project with over 80 participating organizations worldwide, which was responsible for defining the nature of XML retrieval, and how it should be evaluated. Her research is concerned with developing innovative models and metrics of user engagement, through the study of user behavior, web analytics, the analysis of users' emotion and attention, and mouse and gaze movement. She is studying user engagement in areas such as advertising, digital media, social media, and search, and across devices (desktop, tablet and mobile). She also pursue research in social media and search.

HEATHER O'BRIEN

Heather O'Brien is an Assistant Professor at the University of British Columbia whose focus is user engagement with technology. She has explored the conceptual nature of engagement to isolate key attributes of an engaging experience, developed a survey instrument to evaluate users' perceptions of their engagement, and is currently examining the manifestation of engagement and how to measure it in information rich contexts such as online news and search systems. Her research, which has appeared in the Journal of the American Society of Information Science and Technology, Information Processing and Management, Interacting with Computers and various conference proceedings, is supported by the Social Sciences and Humanities Research Council of Canada (SSHRC) and the Networks of Centers of Excellence Graphics and New Media Project (NCE GRAND).

ELAD YOM-TOV

Elad Yom-Tov is a Senior Researcher at Microsoft Research. Before joining Microsoft he was with Yahoo Research, IBM Research, and Rafael. Dr. Yom-Tov studied at Tel-Aviv University and the Technion, Israel. He has published two books, over 60 papers (of which 3 were awarded prizes), and filed more than 30 patents (15 of which have been granted so far). His primary research interests are in large-scale Machine Learning, Information Retrieval, and Social Analysis. He is a Senior Member of IEEE and held the title of Master Inventor while at IBM.

Index

A/B testing, 48
absence time, 58, 62, 63
activity pattern metric, 63
advertizing, 55
aesthetics, 5
aligning eye gaze and mouse movement, 39
Arousal-Valence model, 33

beyond desktop, 61
beyond single site, 61
beyond single task, 61
bucket testing, 48

cardiovascular measures, 32
characteristics of user engagement, 4
click depth, 55
clickthrough rate, 55
cognitive absorption, 29
combining approaches, 73
conversion rate as a measure of engagement, 56
CTR, 55
cumulative activity metric, 63
cursor tracking, 38

dimensions of online measurements, 48
dimensions of user engagement measurement, 8
direct value measurement, 57
downstream engagement score, 65
dwell time, 52

electroencephalogram (EEG), 32
electromyographic (EMG) sensors, 33
endurability, 5
eye tracking, 35

facial expression, 34
focus attention, 4
functional magnetic resonance imaging (fMRI), 32

inter-session engagement, 47
inter-session engagement measures, 56
interview, 15
intra-session engagement, 47
intra-session versus inter-session engagement, 47

large-scale measurements of user engagement, 50

mental workload, 27
methodology bias, 13
mouse movement, 38
mouse tracking, 56
mutitasking, 54

network of sites, 65
networked user engagement, 64
news aggregators, 53
novelty, 5

objectivity versus subjectivity, 8

online multitasking, 61

page view, 55
physiological measures, 31
play time, 53
playfullness, 28
Plutchik's wheel of emotions, 45
positive affect, 4
product-based versus process-based
        measurement, 9
psychophysiological measures, 32
pupillometry, 33

questionnaires, 20

reliability and validity, 14
reputation, trust and expectation, 6
respiratory sensors, 33
return-rate measurements, 58
revenue as a measure of engagement, 57
richness and control, 6

scale, 8
self-report methods, 11
semi-structured interview, 15

setting, 8
site revisits, 54
skin conductance level (SCL), 33
social media, 53
social network, 57
structured interview, 15
survey to evaluate engagement (SEE), 22

think after protocols, 18
think aloud protocols, 18
total use measurements, 57

unstructured interview, 15
usage time, 57
user context, motivation, incentives and
        benefits, 7
user engagement in the mobile context, 68
User Engagement Scale (UES), 24
user engagement versus user experience, 3

video, 53

web analytics, 47
WEIRD, 90

Printed in the United States
by Baker & Taylor Publisher Services